PIANO ACCOMPANIMENT BOOK 1

ESSENTIAL ELEMENTS for Strings

COMPREHENSIVE STRING METHOD

MICHAEL ALLEN • ROBERT GILLESPIE • PAMELA TELLEJOHN HAYES
ARRANGEMENTS BY JOHN HIGGINS

These piano accompaniments can provide helpful guidance for teaching beginning string players. The format includes a cue line to provide the teacher or pianist with a visual guide of the student melody part.

The accompaniments have been arranged to match the style and harmony of the accompaniments heard on Essential Elements Interactive (www.essentialelementsinteractive.com). They may be used for teaching or performance and offer a variety of styles, from classical to contemporary popular music. You may want to alter these piano accompaniments to meet your specific needs. Chord symbols are provided.

ISBN 979-835013653-1

1. TUNING TRACK

2. LET'S PLAY "OPEN D"

3. LET'S PLAY "OPEN A"

4. TWO'S A TEAM

5. AT PIERROT'S DOOR

6. JUMPING JACKS
pizz.
D5 A5 D5 A5 Csus2 D5
7. MIX 'EM UP
pizz.
D7 G9 C13 D7 G9 E7 G/A D7
8. COUNT CAREFULLY
Student books have repeats, not 1st and 2nd endings (until ex. 76).
pizz.
1. 2.
G(add9) D/F♯ G(add9) D/F♯ G(add9) G/A D G(add9) G/A D
9. ESSENTIAL ELEMENTS QUIZ
Student books have repeats, not 1st and 2nd endings (until ex. 76).
pizz.
1. 2.
D A/C♯ G/B A/C♯ D Bmi7 D/A G Emi7 D G/A G Emi7 D

10. LET'S READ "G"

11. LET'S READ "F♯" (F-sharp)

12. LIFT OFF

13. ON THE TRAIL
Student books have repeats, not 1st and 2nd endings (until ex. 76).
pizz.
1.
2.
G D C D G D C D G C D G C G
14. LET'S READ "G"
pizz.
C Ami7 Fma7 G6 C
15. WALKING SONG
Student books have repeats, not 1st and 2nd endings (until ex. 76).
pizz.
1.
2.
G7 B7 C7 D7 C7 D7 C7 G7 C7 G7
16. ESSENTIAL ELEMENTS QUIZ
pizz.
G D/G C/G D/G G/B C D Gsus G

17. HOP SCOTCH

pizz.
G D C D G D C D C7 G

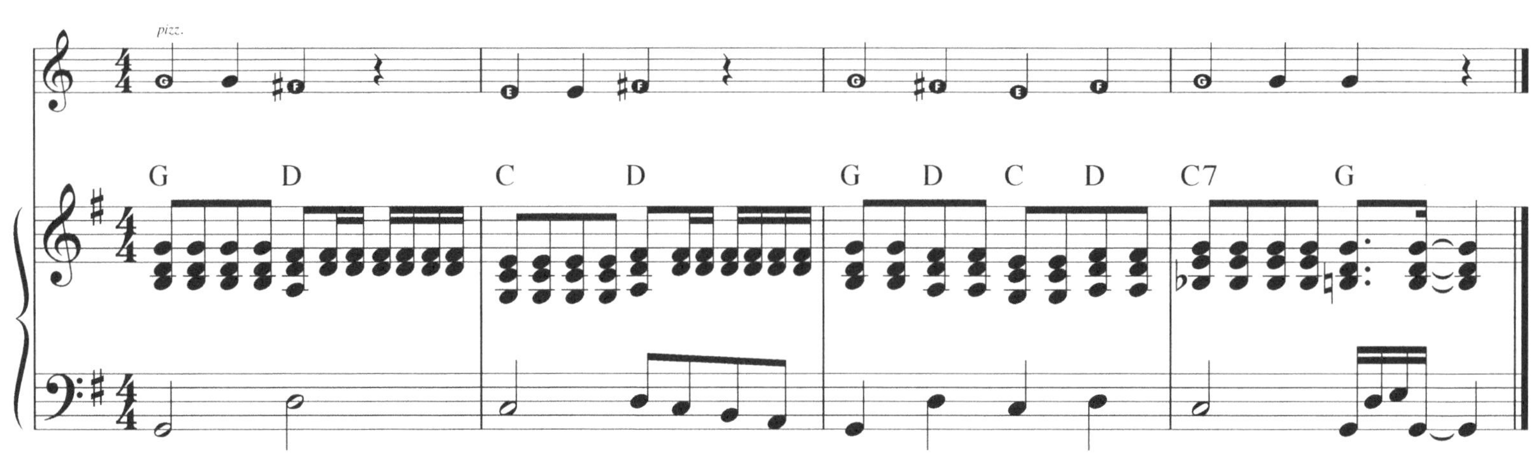

18. MORNING DANCE

Slavic Folk Song

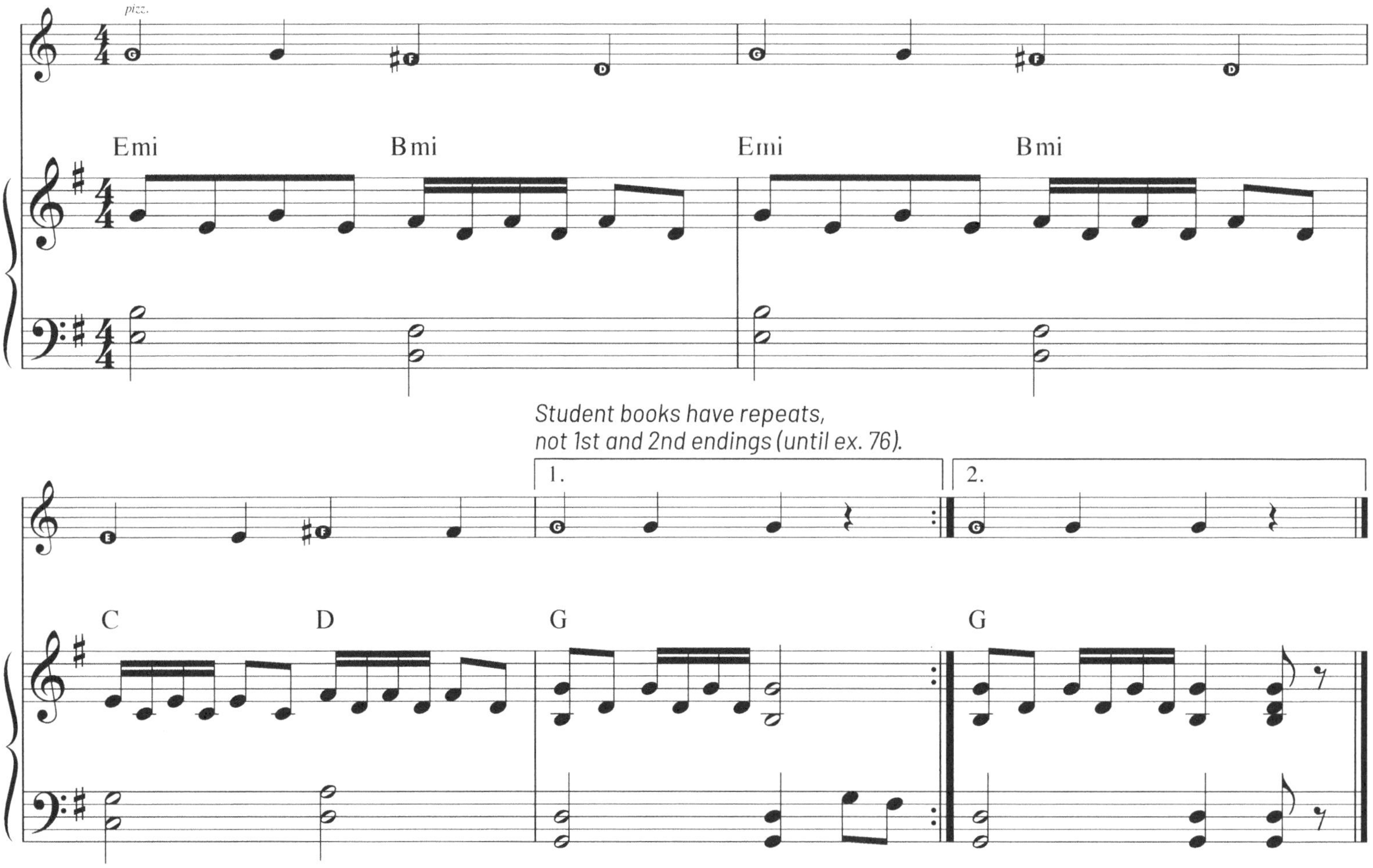

pizz.
Emi Bmi Emi Bmi
Student books have repeats, not 1st and 2nd endings (until ex. 76).
1.
2.
C D G G

19. ROLLING ALONG

20. GOOD KING WENCESLAS

Student books have repeats, not 1st and 2nd endings (until ex. 76).

Welsh Folk Song

21. SEMINOLE CHANT

Student books have repeats, not 1st and 2nd endings (until ex. 76).

22. ESSENTIAL ELEMENTS QUIZ – LIGHTLY ROW

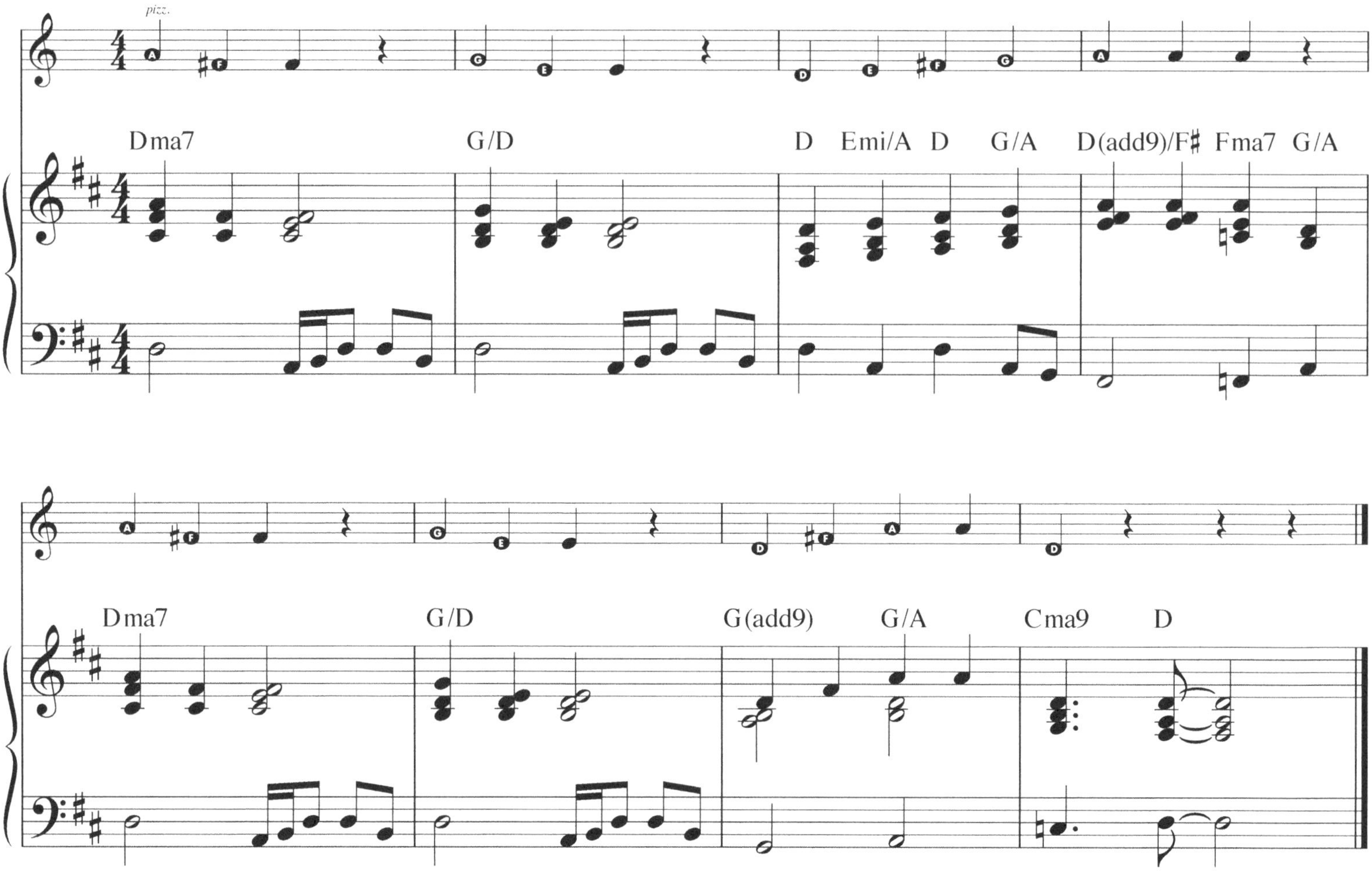
pizz.
Dma7
G/D
D Emi/A D G/A
D(add9)/F♯ Fma7 G/A
Dma7
G/D
G(add9) G/A
Cma9 D

23. LET'S READ "D"

pizz.
D(add9)
G(add9)
F6 G(add9)
D(add9)

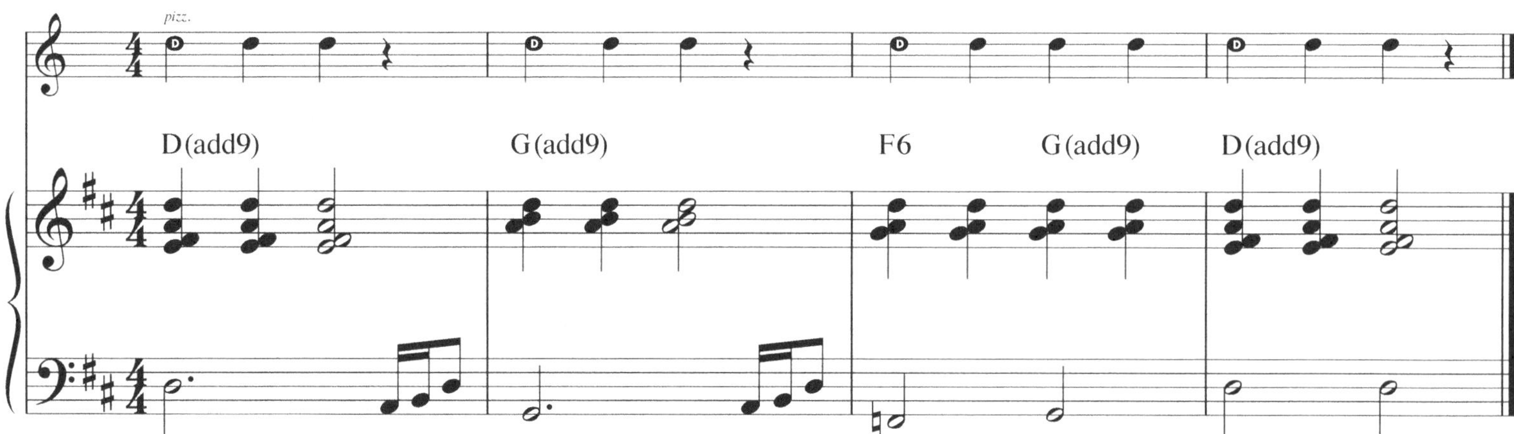

24. LET'S READ "C♯" (C-sharp)

25. TAKE OFF

26. CARIBBEAN ISLAND

27. OLYMPIC HIGH JUMP

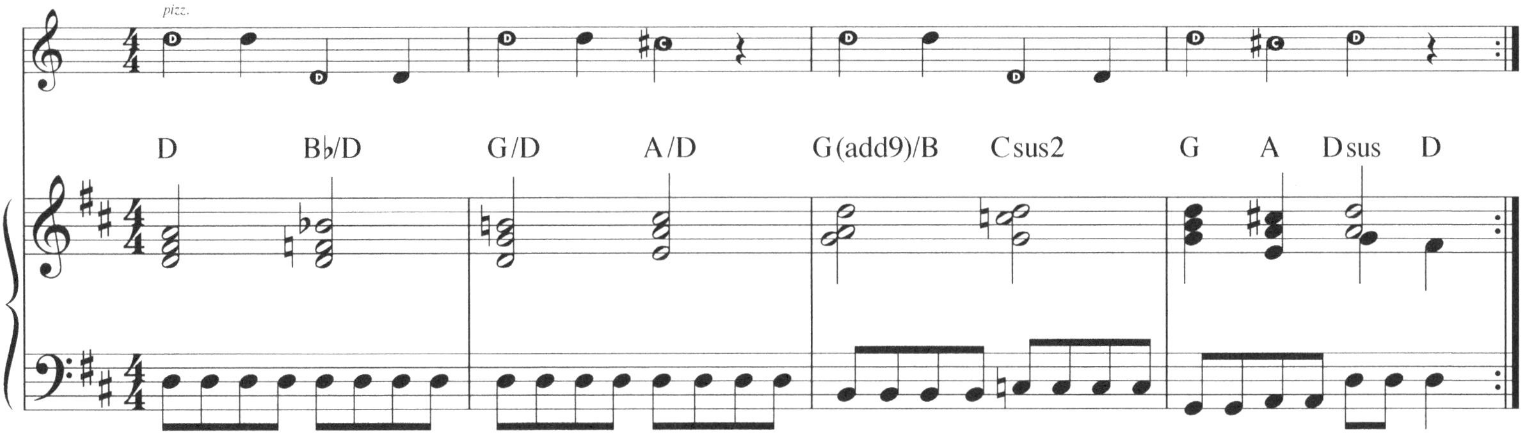
pizz.
D Bb/D G/D A/D G(add9)/B Csus2 G A Dsus D

28. LET'S READ "B"

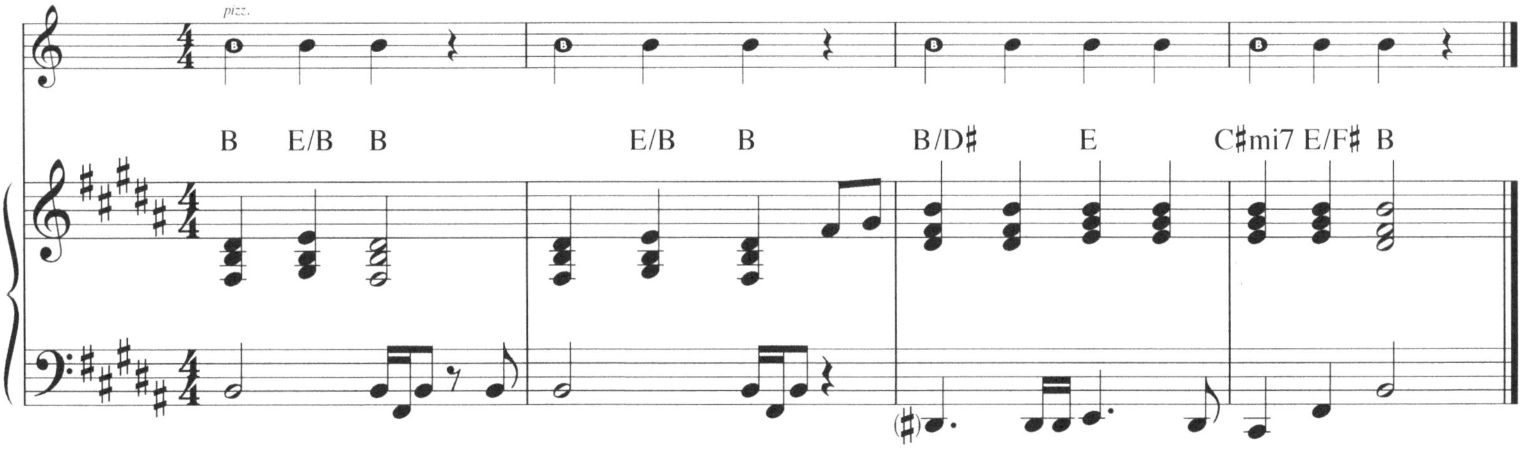
pizz.
B E/B B E/B B B/D# E C#mi7 E/F# B

29. HALF WAY DOWN

pizz.
D A G D A D

30. RIGHT BACK UP

pizz.
A G/A A G A/G Dsus D

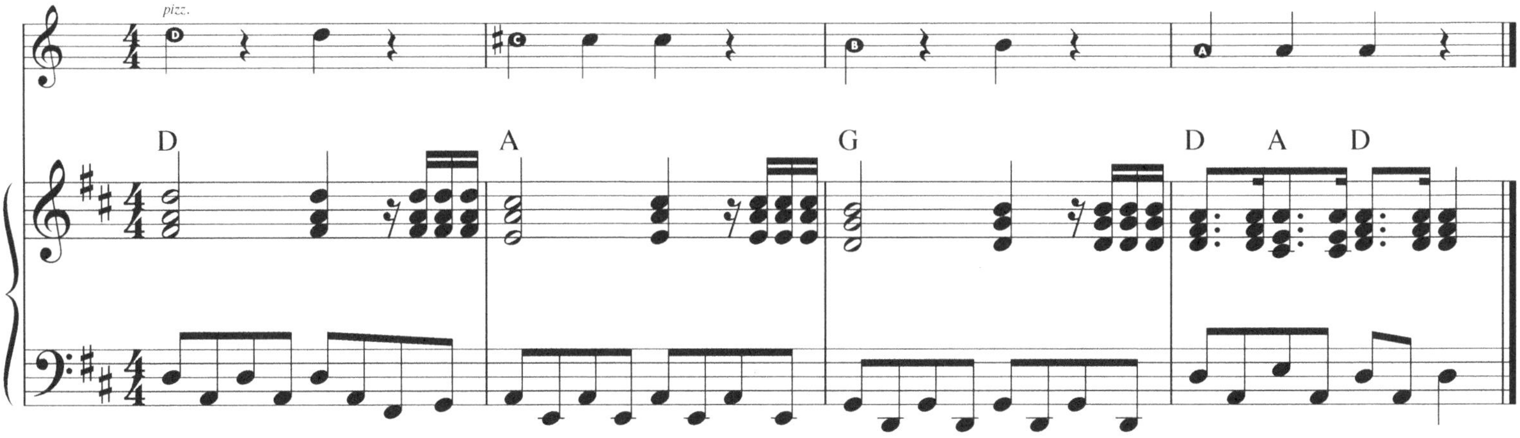

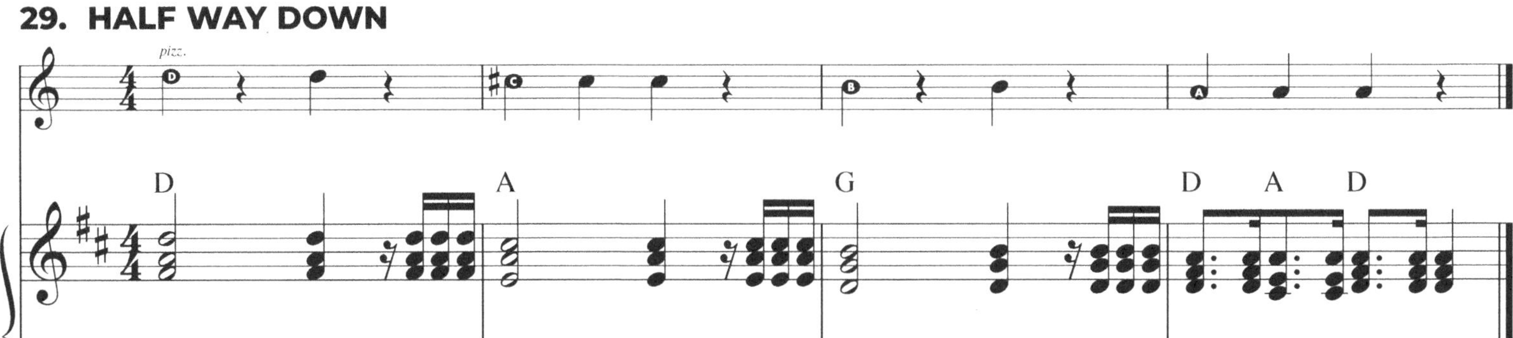

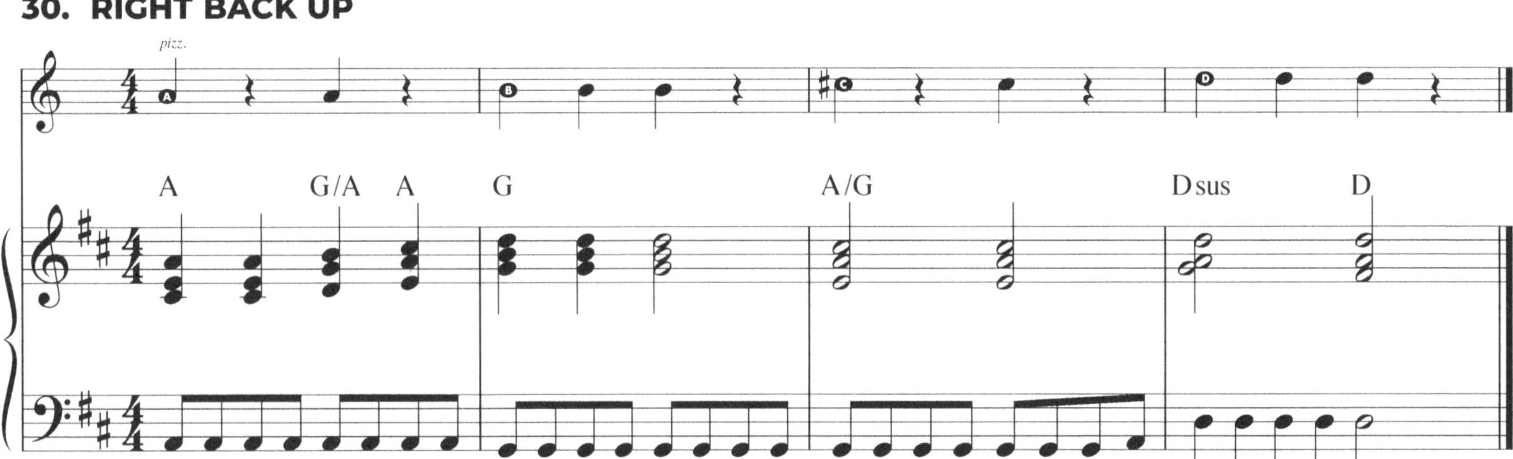

31. DOWN THE D SCALE
pizz.
D
F♯mi
G
F♯mi
G
D/A
Emi/A
D
32. ESSENTIAL ELEMENTS QUIZ – UP THE D SCALE
pizz.
D
A
D
G
D
G
A
G
D

35. ESSENTIAL CREATIVITY – *writing assignment in student books*

36. DREIDEL

Israeli Folk Song

37. ROSIN RAP #1

Student books have repeats, not 1st and 2nd endings (until ex. 76).

38. ROSIN RAP #2

Student books have repeats, not 1st and 2nd endings (until ex. 76).

39. ROSIN RAP #3

Student books have repeats, not 1st and 2nd endings (until ex. 76).

40. CAROLINA BREEZE

Student books have repeats, not 1st and 2nd endings (until ex. 76).

41. JINGLE BELLS

J. S. Pierpont

42. OLD MACDONALD HAD A FARM

American Folk Song

pizz.

G C G A7 D7 G

G7 C G C G

G C G A7 D7 G D7 G

43. A MOZART MELODY

Adapted by W. A. Mozart

44. MATTHEW'S MARCH

46. ESSENTIAL CREATIVITY – *writing assignment in student books*

47. BOW ON THE D STRING

49. RAISE AND LOWER
Student books have a repeat in measure 4.
Raise your arm.
Lower your arm.
A7 G(add9)/B Cmi6 A7/C♯
D7 C(add9)/E Fmi6 D7/F♯
Raise your arm.
Lower your arm.
G/A F♯mi/A Emi/A D/A A7
G/A F♯mi/A Emi/A D/A
D
50. TEETER TOTTER
Asus
D5
Asus
D5
C5 D5
51. MIRROR IMAGE
D/A
A7sus
Bmi Bmi/A G♯mi7(♭5)
G A/G
D/A
G Emi7 D

52. A STRAND OF D 'N' A
G(add9) D/F♯ Dsus/E D/F♯ G(add9) D/F♯ E7 G/A D
53. ESSENTIAL ELEMENTS QUIZ – OLYMPIC CHALLENGE
Dsus2 Dsus2/G Dsus2/F Dsus2/G Dsus2
54. BOWING "G"
G C/G Csus/G C G
55. BACK AND FORTH
G(add9) D9 D7(♭9) G(add9) Bmi7 Cma7 D7(♭9) G(add9)

56. DOWN AND UP
G B7 C D7 G B7 C D7 G
57. TRIBAL LAMENT
Student books have repeats, not 1st and 2nd endings (until ex. 76).
1.
2.
E5 D/E E5 D/E Emi D/E Emi Emi
58. BOWING "D"
D Bmi G A/G G D/A A7sus G Emi7 D
59. LITTLE STEPS
D A G A G A D

60. ELEVATOR DOWN

61. ELEVATOR UP

62. DOWN THE D MAJOR SCALE

63. SCALE SIMULATOR

65. LET'S READ "C♯" – Review
A
G
A
D
66. RHYTHM RAP
D
A7
G
D
G
D
A7
D
67. PEPPERONI PIZZA
D
A7
G
D
G
D
A7
D
68. RHYTHM RAP
D
Emi7/A
D/F♯
C
Dma7/A
Emi7/A
A7
D

69. D MAJOR SCALE UP

70. HOT CROSS BUNS

Student books have repeats, not 1st and 2nd endings (until ex. 76).

71. AU CLAIRE DE LA LUNE

French Folk Song

72. RHYTHM RAP

Student books have a repeat sign in measure 4.

73. BUCKEYE SALUTE

74. RHYTHM RAP
Dsus D A/D G/D D Emi/A G/A Bmi7 A Dsus D
75. TWO BY TWO
Dsus D A/D G/D D Emi/A G/A Bmi7 A Dsus D
76. ESSENTIAL ELEMENTS QUIZ – FOR PETE'S SAKE
Moderato
D6/9 Emi7/A Ami7/D
Gma9 C9(♯11) Bmi7 Dma7/A Gma7 A/G D(add2)/F♯

1.
2.
Emi7
A9(♭5)
A7 E♭7(♯9)
G/A A7(♭9) D6/9
77. RHYTHM RAP
Student books have repeats, not 1st and 2nd endings.
1.
2.
D A7 D A7 Bmi Asus A G D/F♯ Emi7 A7 G D/F♯ Emi D
78. AT PIERROT'S DOOR
Student books have repeats, not 1st and 2nd endings.
French Folk Song
Moderato
1.
2.
D A7 D A7 Bmi Asus A G D/F♯ Emi7 A7 G D/F♯ Emi D
79. THE HALF COUNTS
D7 A7 G7 D7 C7 Dma7 B♭7(♭5) A7 G7 D

80. GRANDPARENT'S DAY

American Folk Song

Andante
D Bmi G D/F♯ Bmi7 E9 Gma7 C A7
D D7 G/D G6/9 Emi7(♭5) D/A Bmi7 Gma7 A7 Dsus D

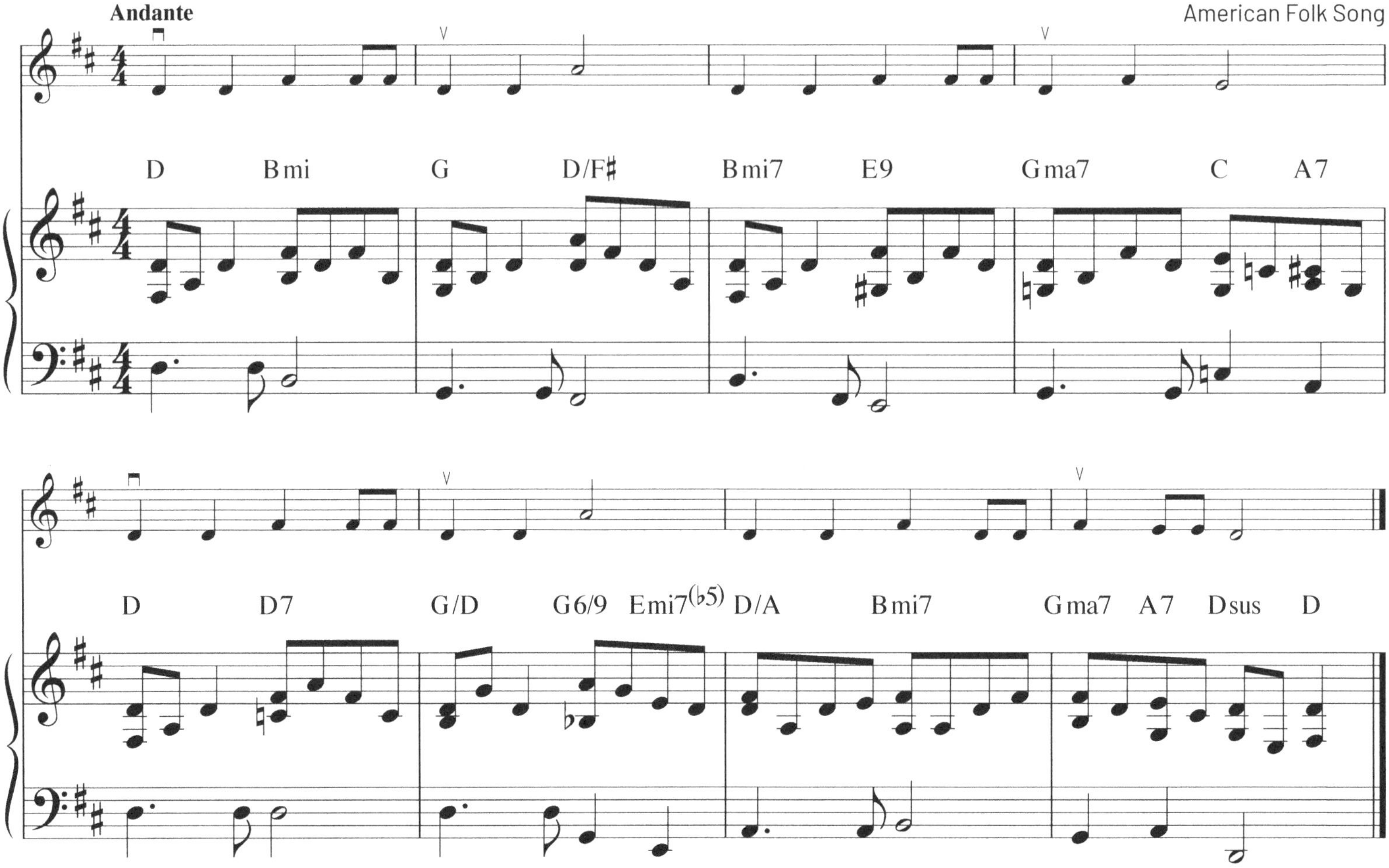

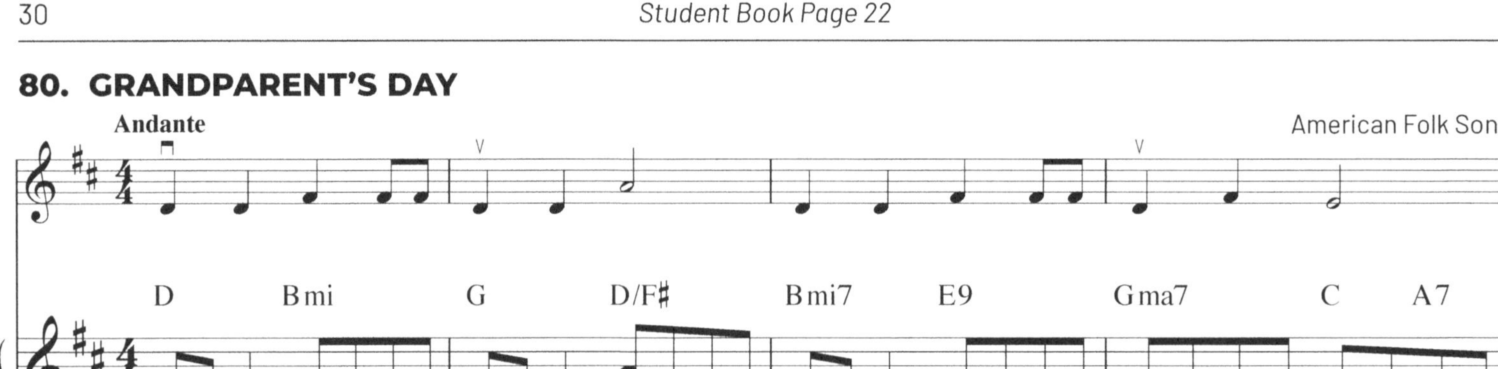

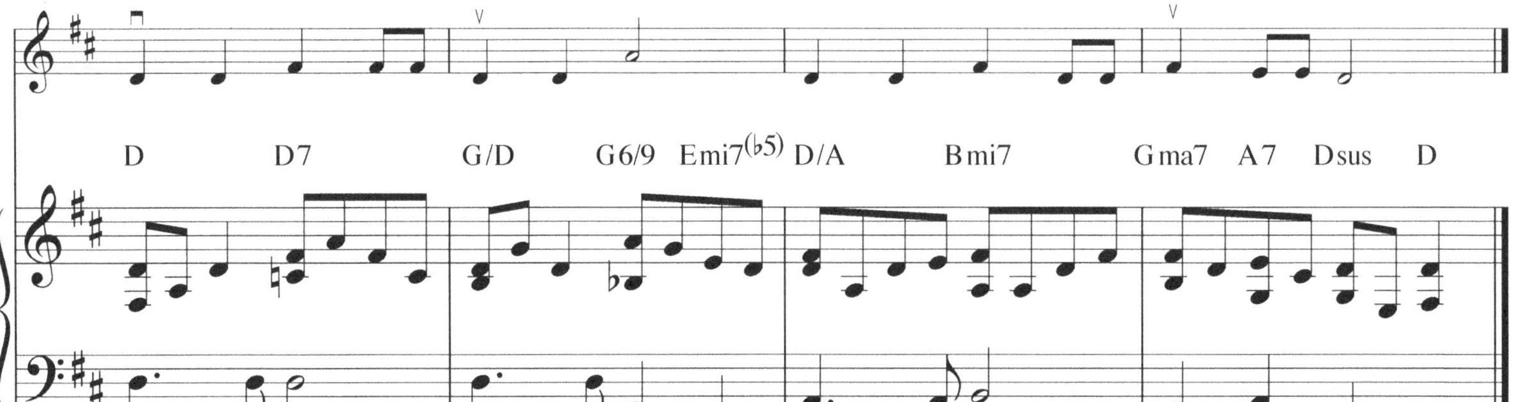

81. MICHAEL ROW THE BOAT ASHORE

American Folk Song

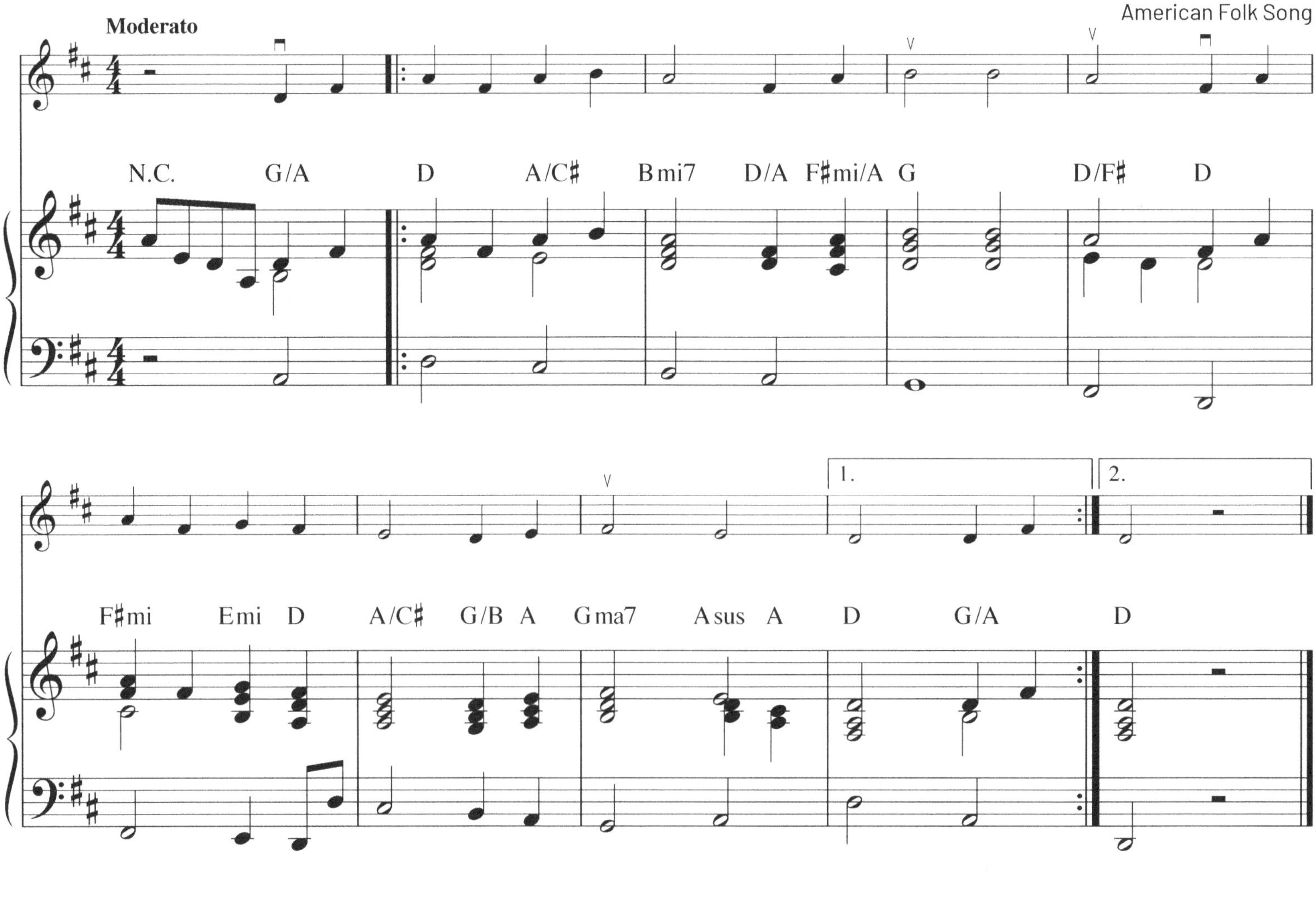

Moderato
N.C. G/A D A/C♯ Bmi7 D/A F♯mi/A G D/F♯ D
1.
2.
F♯mi Emi D A/C♯ G/B A Gma7 Asus A D G/A D

82. TEXAS TWO-STRING

83. FOUR BY FOUR

84. 4TH FINGER MARATHON

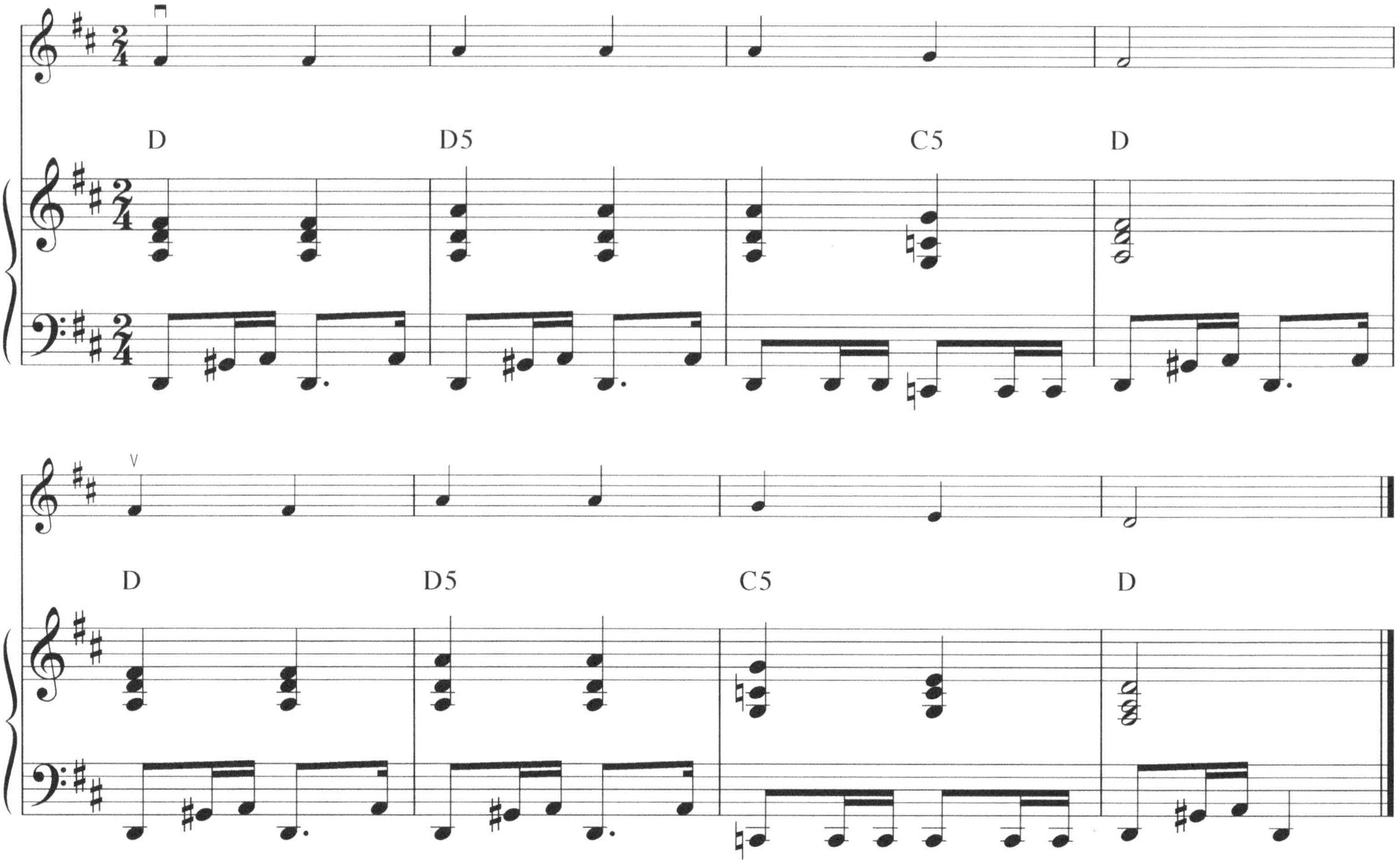
D
D5
C5
D
D
D5
C5
D

85. HIGH FLYING

D
A7
G
Emi
A
D

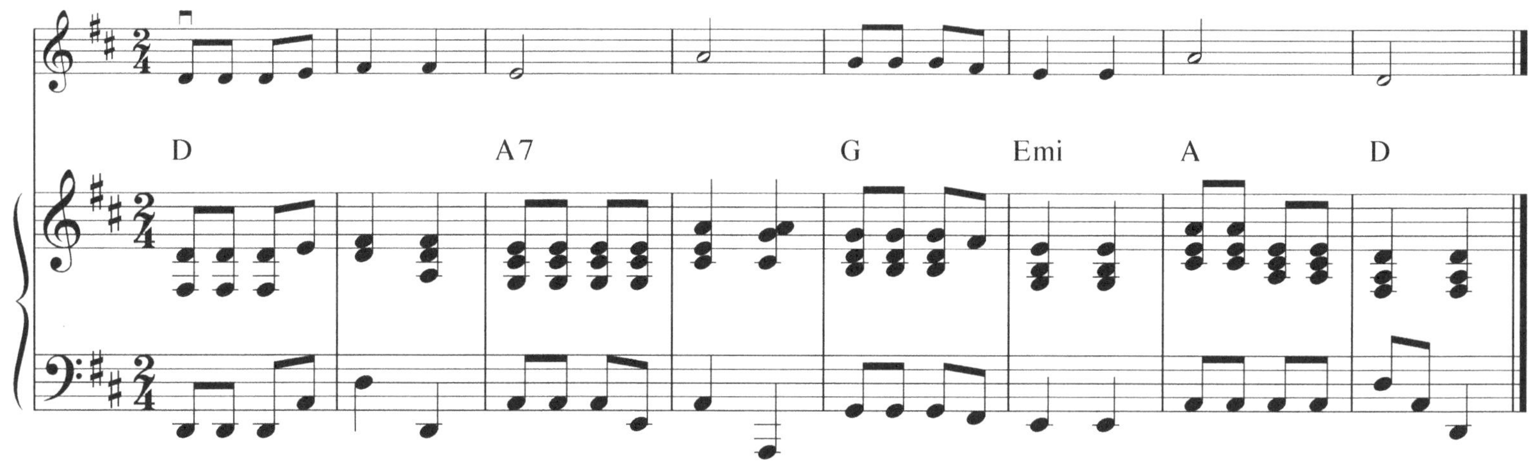

86. ESSENTIAL ELEMENTS QUIZ – ODE TO JOY

87. SCALE WARM-UP

88. FRÈRE JACQUES – Round *(When group A reaches ②, group B begins at ①)*

89. BOIL 'EM CABBAGE DOWN – Orchestra Arrangement

American Fiddle Tune

90. ENGLISH ROUND

91. LIGHTLY ROW – Orchestra Arrangement

Moderato

A

B

D A7 D A D A7 D A D

5

A

B

A A7 D D/F♯ D A7 D A D

92. CAN-CAN – Orchestra Arrangement

Jacques Offenbach
Arr. John Higgins

93. LET'S READ "G"

94. LET'S READ "C" (C-natural)

95. LET'S READ "B"

96. LET'S READ "A"

97. WALKING AROUND

98. G MAJOR SCALE

99. FOURTH FINGER D

100. LOW DOWN

101. BAA BAA BLACK SHEEP

Moderato
G
Bmi7
Cma7
Bmi7
C/D
Bmi/D
Ami/D
G

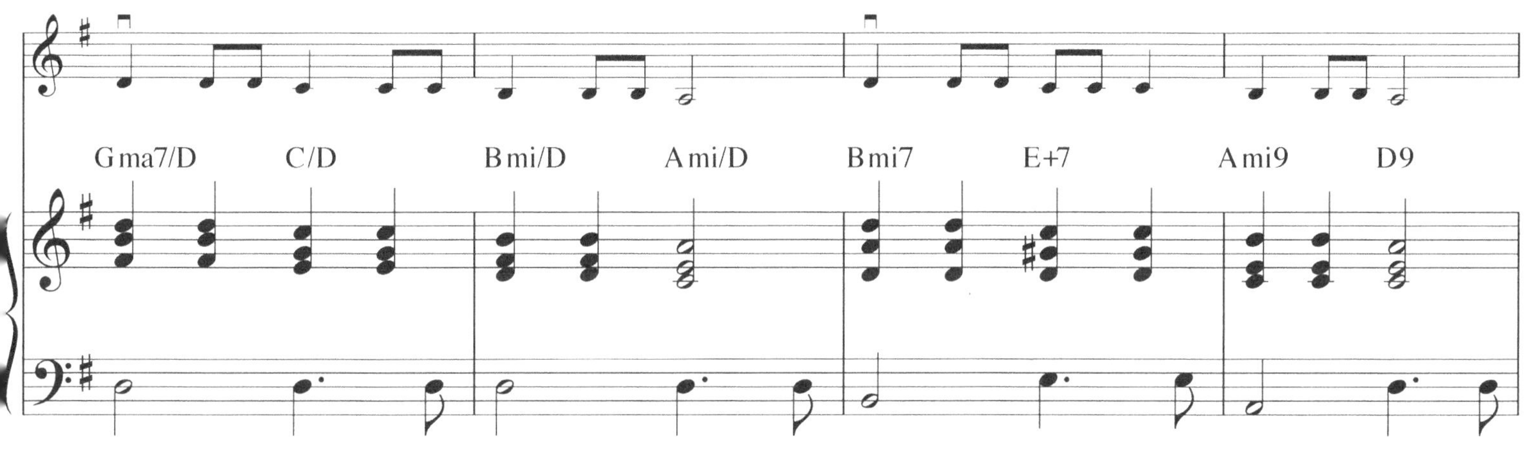
Gma7/D
C/D
Bmi/D
Ami/D
Bmi7
E+7
Ami9
D9

G
Bmi7
Cma7
E9
Ami7
Gma7/D
Ami/D
G

102. ESSENTIAL ELEMENTS QUIZ – THIS OLD MAN
Moderato
American Folk Song
G
C
D7
G
D7
G D7 G
103. RHYTHM RAP
Student books have repeats, not 1st and 2nd endings.
1.
2.
D
A7
D
D/A
D
104. COUNTING THREES
Student books have repeats, not 1st and 2nd endings.
1.
2.
D
A7
D
D/A
D

105. D MAJOR SCALE IN THREES

106. FRENCH FOLK SONG

107. ESSENTIAL ELEMENTS QUIZ – SAILOR'S SONG

108. FIT TO BE TIED

109. STOP AND GO

110. SLURRING ALONG
D Emi/D
Dma7 Emi/D
D Emi/D
Dma7 Emi/D
Gma7
G/A
D C9(♯11)
D
111. SMOOTH SAILING
D A
G D
A Bmi
E9 Asus A
D D/F♯
G E/G♯
G/A
D

112. D MAJOR SLURS
D A7sus A/C♯ D D7 G Emi Asus A
Dma7 Cma7/D Gma7 A/G F♯mi/A G/A A7sus A7 D
113. CROSSING STRINGS
D9 D9/F♯ G13 A9 D9 D9/F♯ G13 A7 D9 N.C.
114. GLIDING BOWS
Bmi7 B♭ma7 Asus A D(add9) F♯mi7 G6 Asus Gmi Ami D

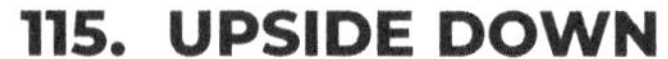

115. UPSIDE DOWN

D(add9) D
Fma7 A7sus
D(add9) D
Fma7 A7sus
B♭ma7 Asus D

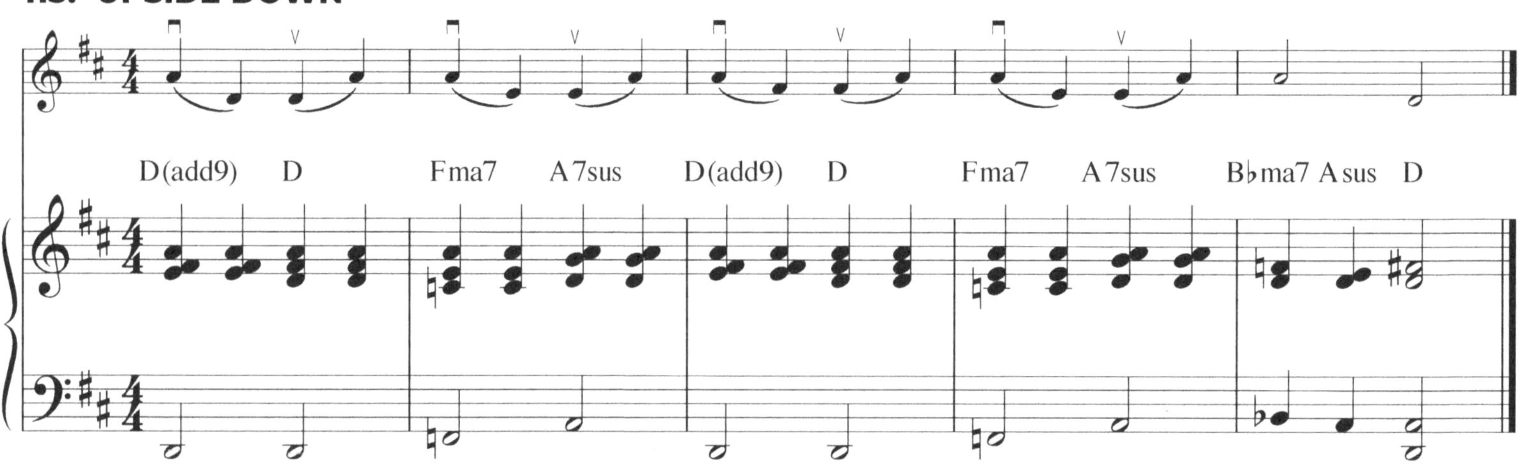

116. SONG FOR MARIA

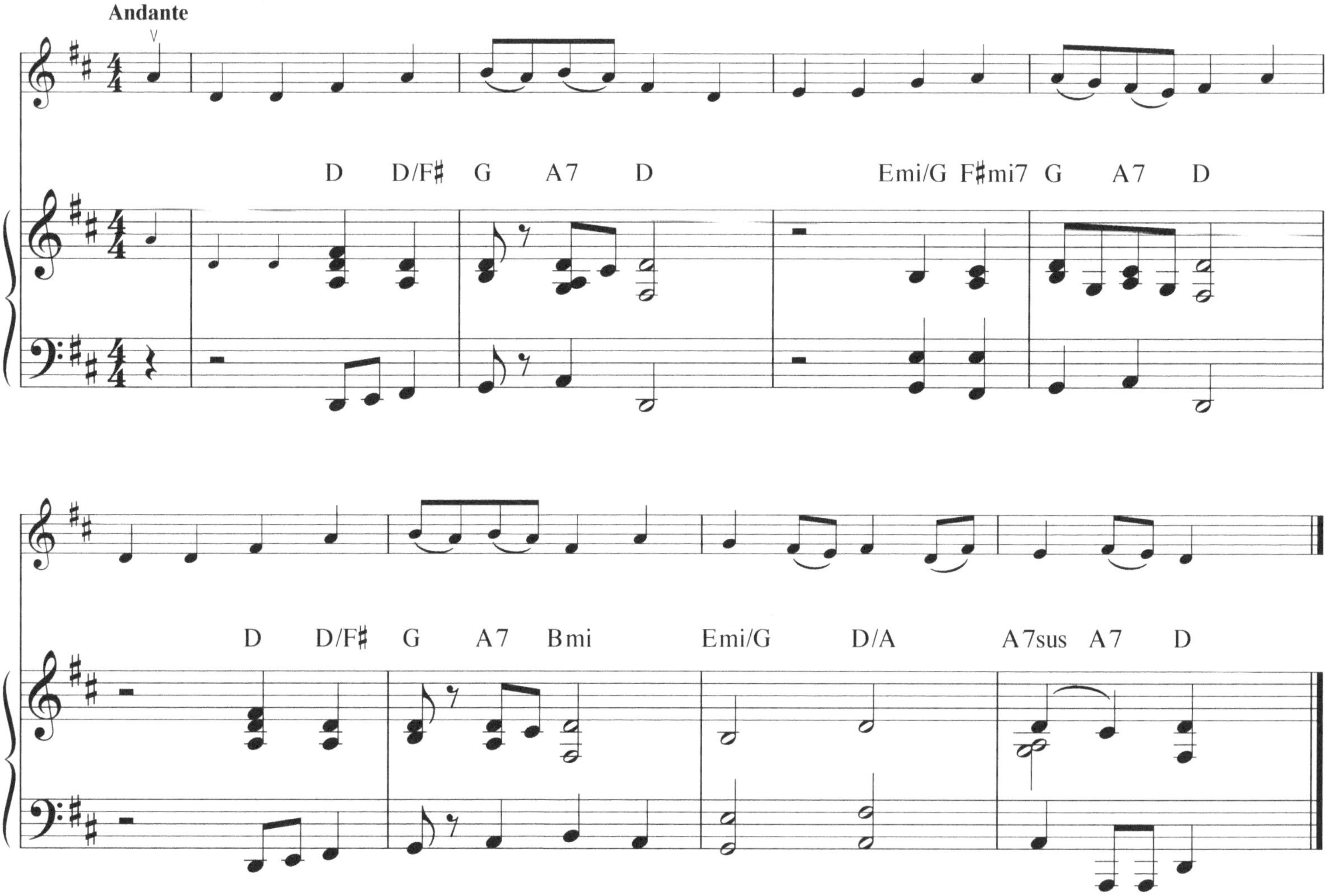

Andante
D D/F♯ G A7 D
Emi/G F♯mi7 G A7 D
D D/F♯ G A7 Bmi
Emi/G D/A
A7sus A7 D

117. BANANA BOAT SONG

Caribbean Folk Song

118. FIROLIRALERA – Orchestra Arrangement
Mexican Folk Song
Arr. John Higgins
Allegro
A
B
D
A7
D
A7
D
G
D/A
A7
D
4

119.

120.

121.
G
G7
C
G
D7
G
122.
G
C
C/D
D7
Emi
Ami
G/B
C6
G/D
C/E
D7/F♯
G
123.
G
Bmi7
C
D7
Emi7
D/C
C
Bmi7
Ami7
D6
D7
G
124.
Emi
Bmi
Ami
Emi
C
D7
C
D7
G

125. JINGLI NONA

Allegro

Far Eastern Folk Song

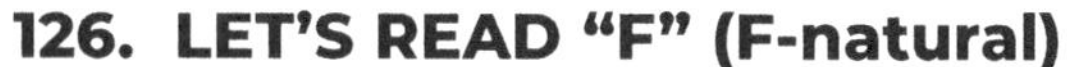

126. LET'S READ "F" (F-natural)

F
F/A
B♭
C
B♭
F

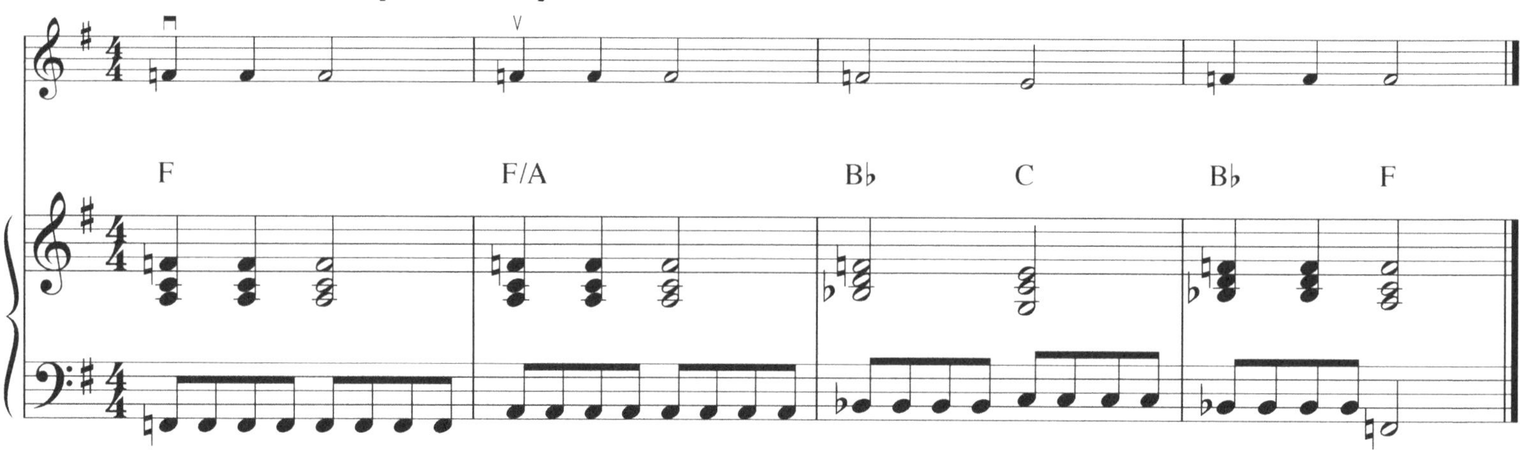

127. HALF-STEPPIN' AND WHOLE-STEPPIN'

Student books have repeats, not 1st and 2nd endings.

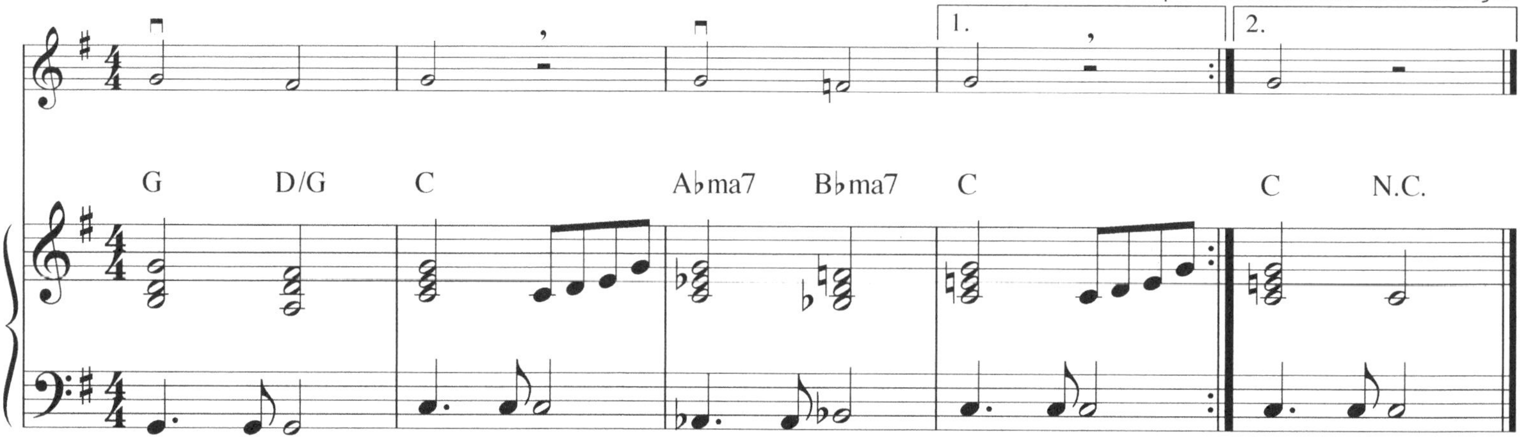
1.
2.
G
D/G
C
A♭ma7
B♭ma7
C
C
N.C.

128. SPY GUY

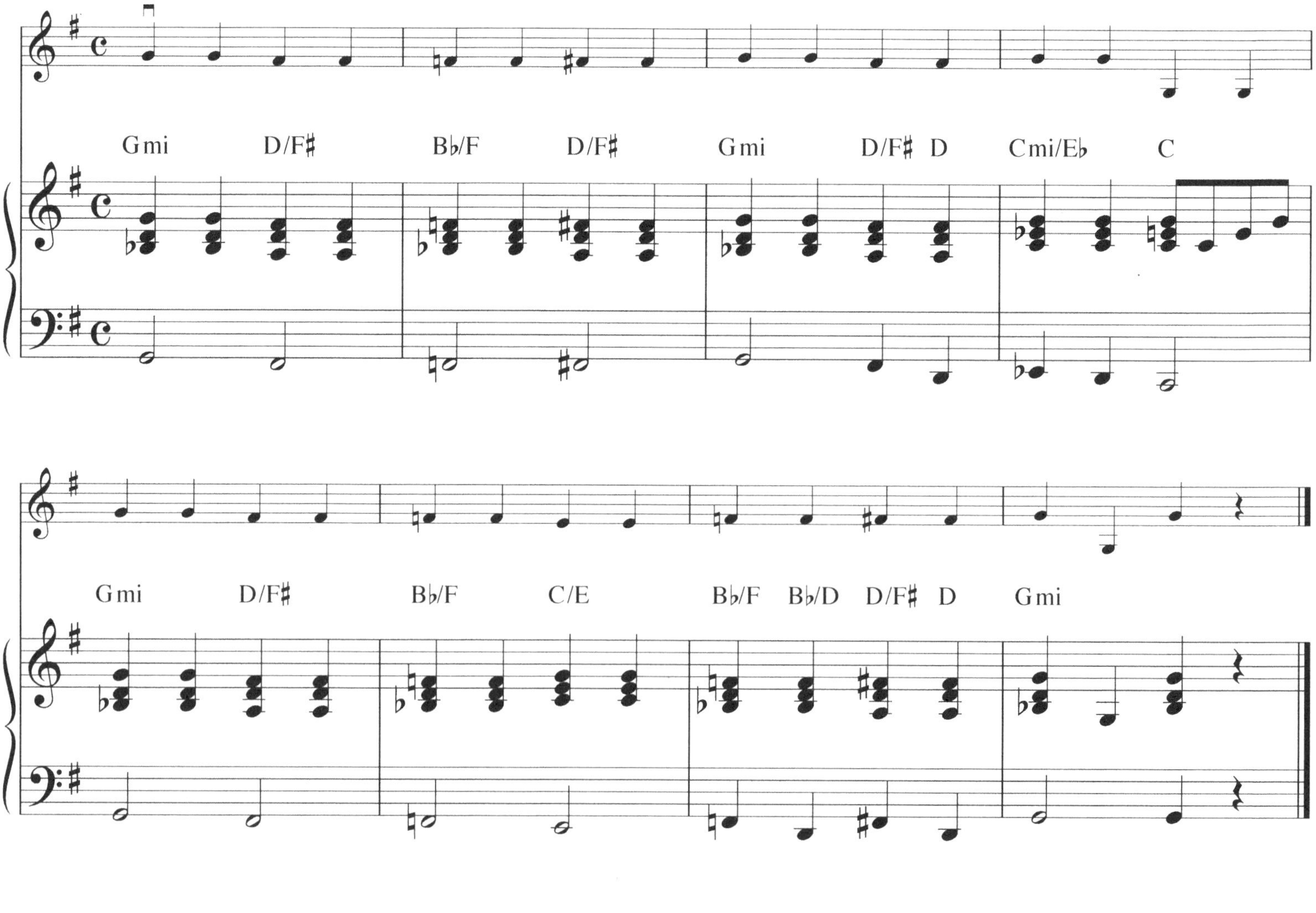
Gmi
D/F♯
B♭/F
D/F♯
Gmi
D/F♯
D
Cmi/E♭
C
Gmi
D/F♯
B♭/F
C/E
B♭/F
B♭/D
D/F♯
D
Gmi

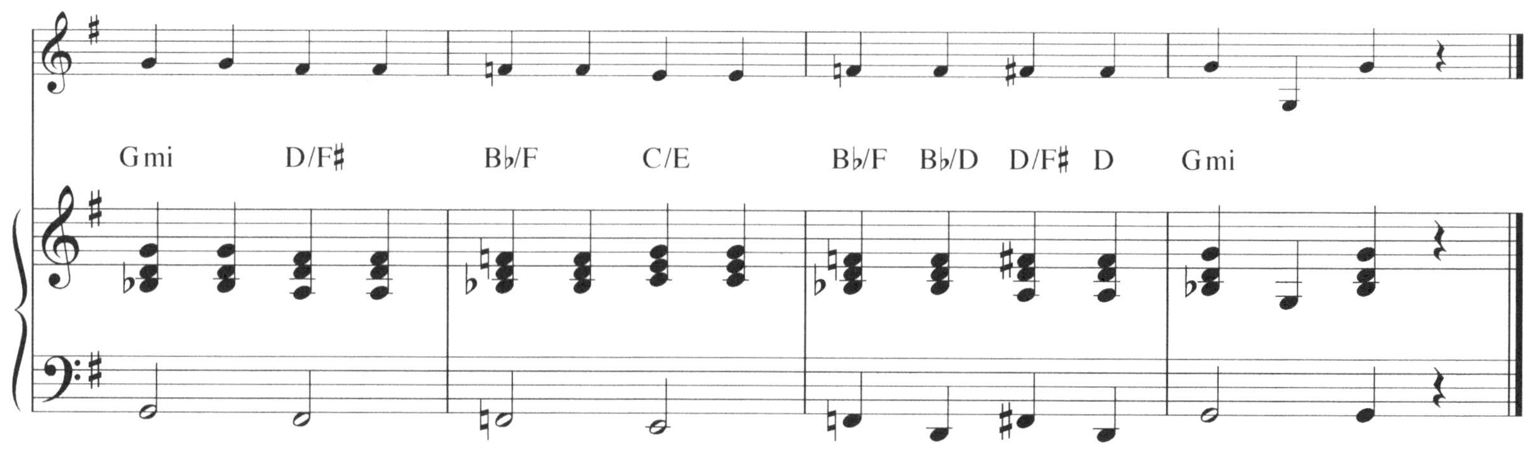

129. MINOR DETAILS

130. LET'S READ "C"

131. HALF STEP AND WHOLE STEP REVIEW

Student books have repeats, not 1st and 2nd endings.

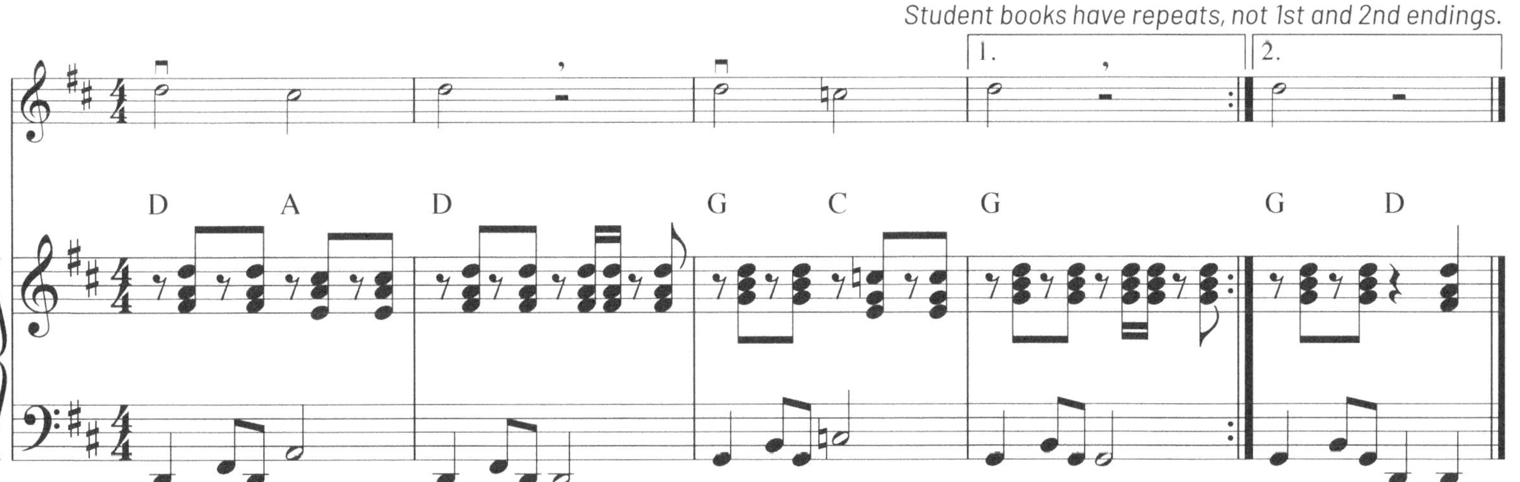

132. CHROMATIC MOVES

133. THE STETSON SPECIAL

134. BLUEBIRD'S SONG

136. SPLIT DECISION – Duet

137. OAK HOLLOW

Moderato

C G7sus C F Dmi F/G Gsus G

C Emi Ami Ami/G F♯mi7(♭5) C/G Ami7 F6/G G6 C

138. A-TISKET, A-TASKET

Allegro

N.C. C F C F C F C

1. 2.

G7sus G G7sus G F G C G7sus C

139. ESSENTIAL ELEMENTS QUIZ – RUSSIAN FOLK TUNE

140. BINGO

18th Century English Game Song

142. VARIATIONS ON A FAMILIAR SONG

Moderato

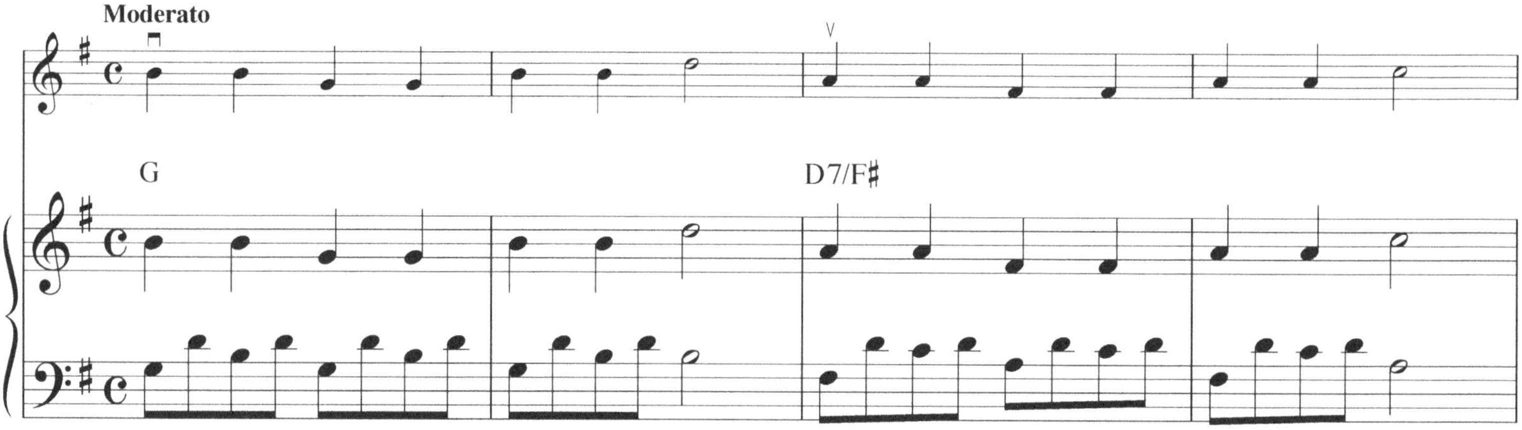
G
D7/F♯

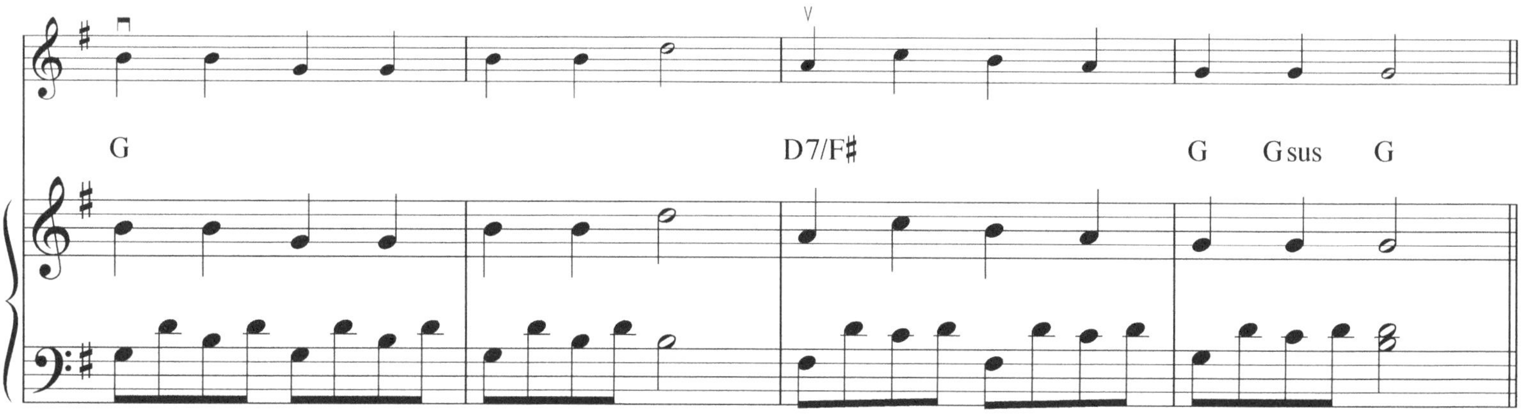
G
D7/F♯
G Gsus G

Variation 1

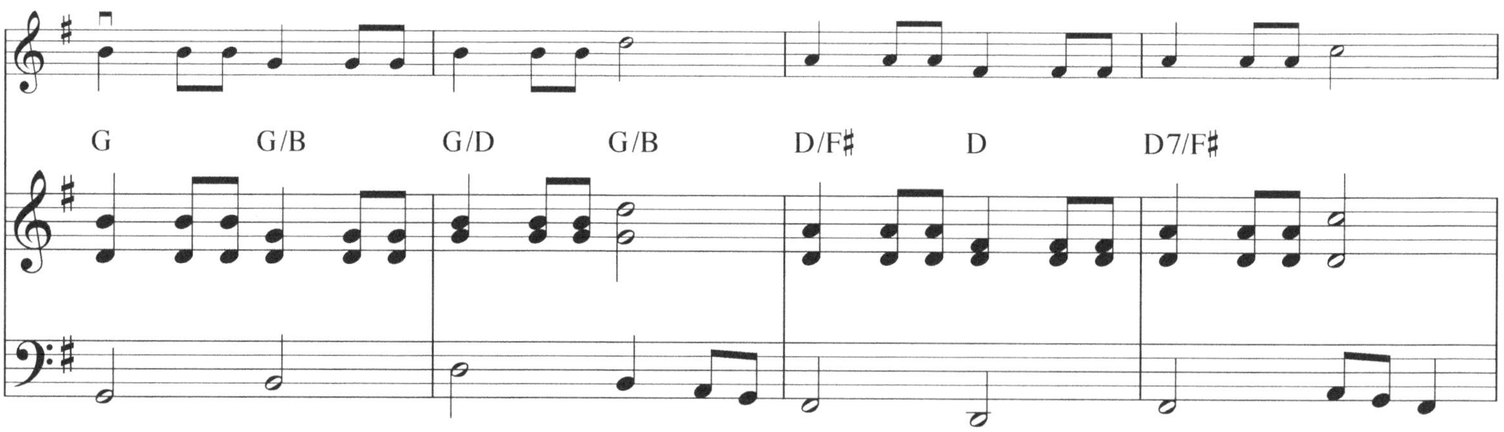
G G/B G/D G/B D/F♯ D D7/F♯

G G/B G/D G7/B Ami/C Ami G/D D7 G

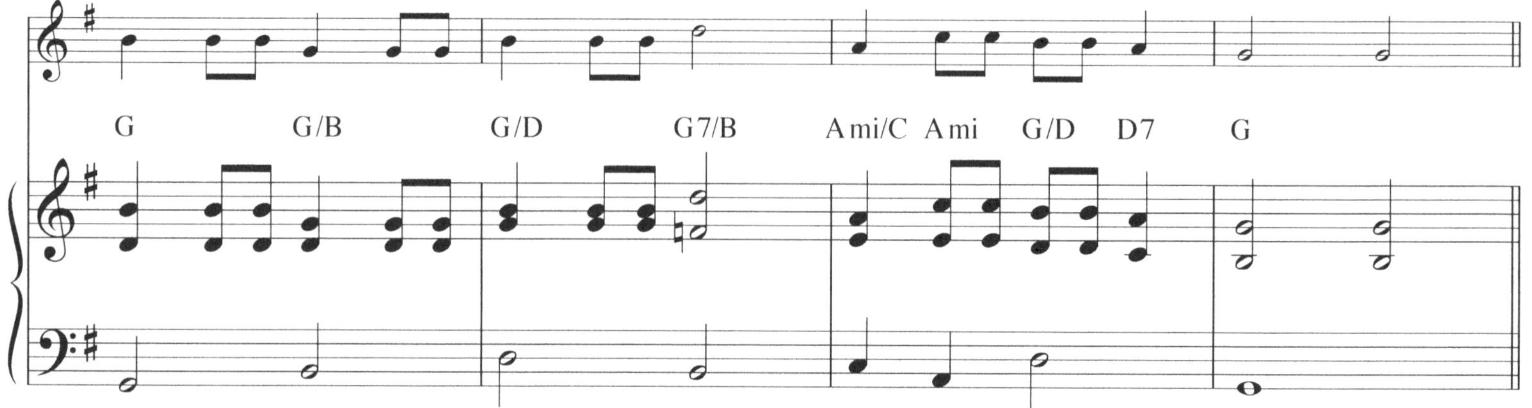

Variation 2 – *make up your own variation*

143. ESSENTIAL CREATIVITY – BIRTHDAY SONG

Student *Now play the line again and create your own rhythm.*

144. LET'S READ "C" – Review

145. LET'S READ "F" – Review

146. LET'S READ "E" – Review

147. LET'S READ "D" – Review

148. SIDE BY SIDE

F C7/E Dmi F/C Ami/C

B♭/C B♭/D C7/E Fsus F

149. C MAJOR SCALE

C G/B F/A Emi/G F C/G Dmi7 G7 C

C Csus/D C/E Fmi/A♭ C/G F/G G7 C

150. RHYTHM RAP
Dmi A/C♯ B♭ F/A C F
151. SLOW BOWS
Dmi A/C♯ B♭ F/A C F
152. LONG LONG AGO
Moderato
T. H. Baily
C F/G C F/G C F/G C G7sus F/G G7sus C/G G7sus C B♭ F/G
C F/G C F/G C F/G C G7sus F/G G7sus Fsus/B♭ C

153. C MAJOR SCALE AND ARPEGGIO

154. LISTEN TO OUR SECTIONS

155. MONDAY'S MELODY

156. LET'S READ "E"
E7 A7 E7 A7 E7
157. LET'S READ "A"
A D A E A
158. LET'S READ "G"
G5 F/G G F/G G
159. LET'S READ "F♯" (F-sharp)
F♯sus F♯ F♯sus2 F♯ Gsus G Bsus B C D Gsus G

160. MOVING ALONG

161. G MAJOR SCALE

162. SHEPHERD'S HEY
Moderato
English Folk Song
D5 Emi/D D Dsus A7 D5 D5/C G/B G/B♭ D/A A7sus D
163. BIG ROCK CANDY MOUNTAIN
Allegro
American Folk Song
A7 D A7 D A7 D A7 D A7
1.
2.
D A7 D A7 D A7
D A7 D A7 D G D

164. LET'S READ "B"

165. ICE SKATING

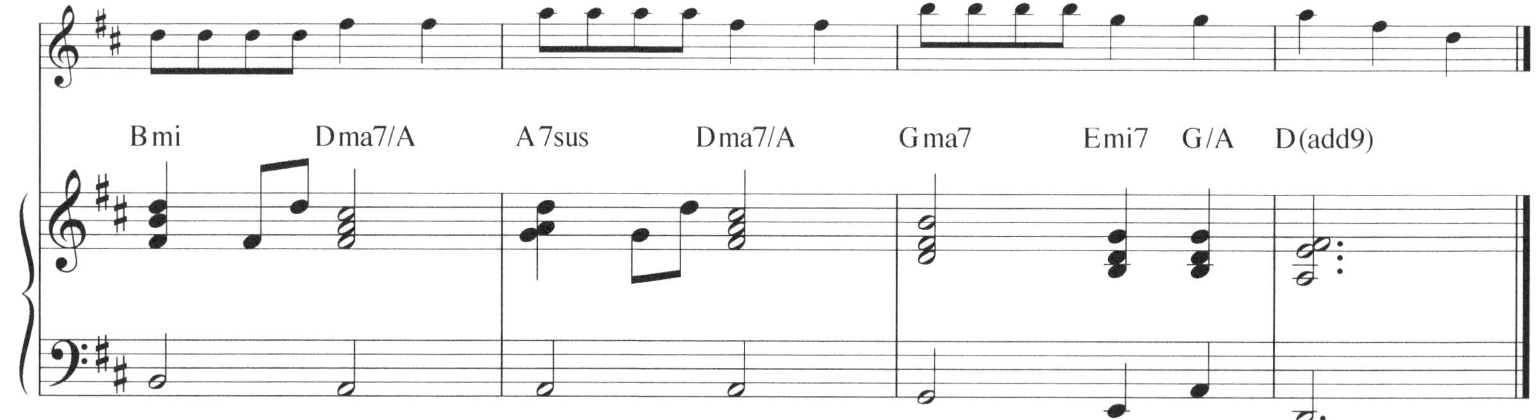

166. ESSENTIAL ELEMENTS QUIZ – ACADEMIC FESTIVAL OVERTURE THEME

Johannes Brahms

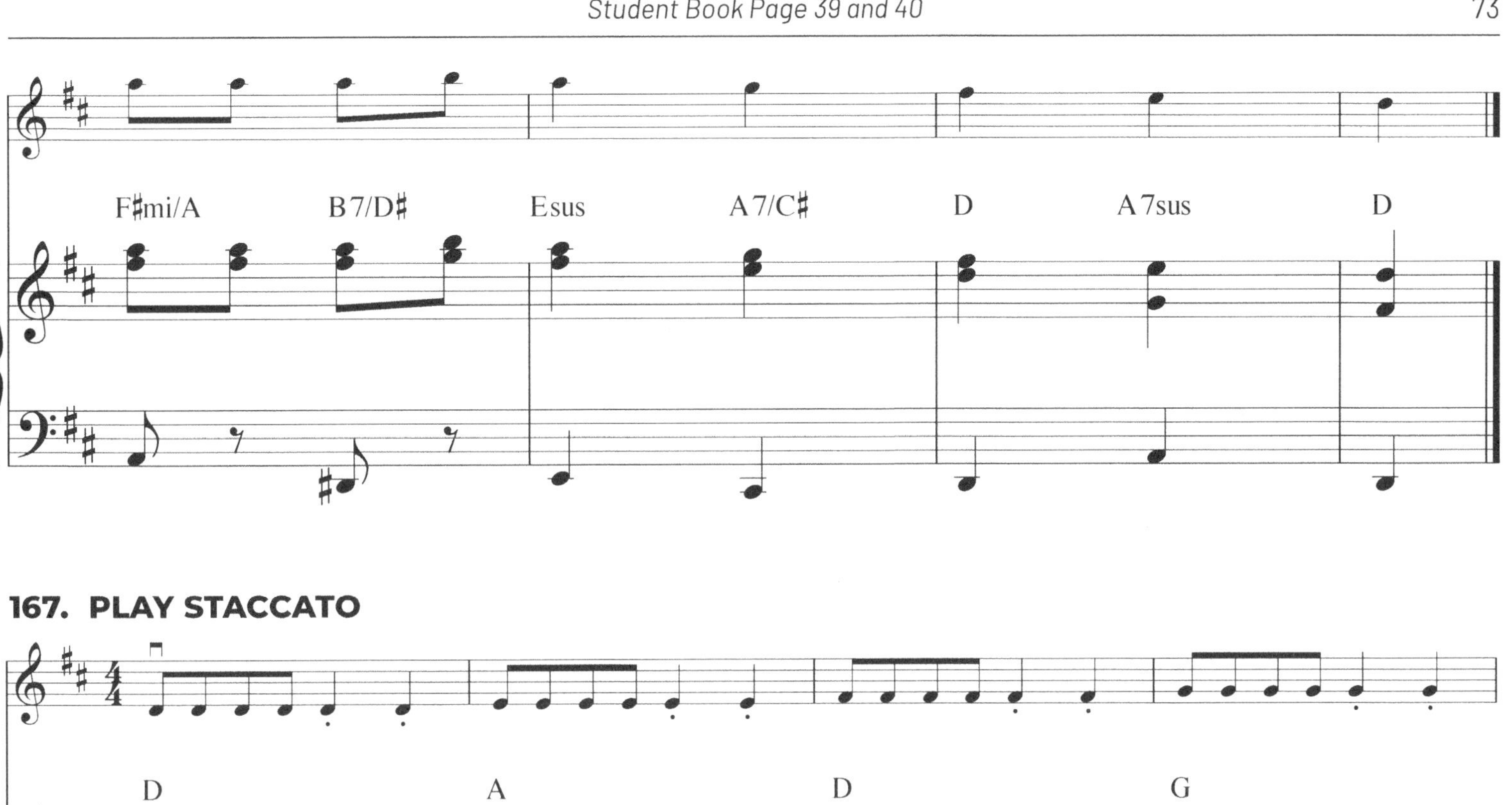

167. PLAY STACCATO

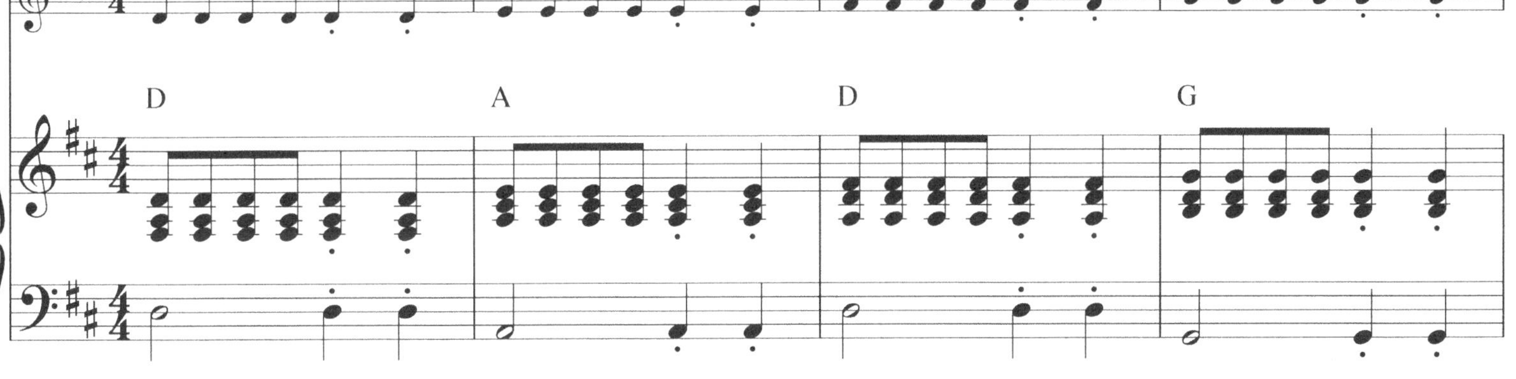

168. ARKANSAS TRAVELER

Southern American Folk Song

Allegro
D
G
D
E
E7
A7
D
G
D
G
D/A
A7
D

169.

G
C/G
D/F♯
Emi
G/D
C
Ami7
Ami7/D
Gsus G

170.

G
B7
G7
C
A7
D7
E7
A7
D7
G

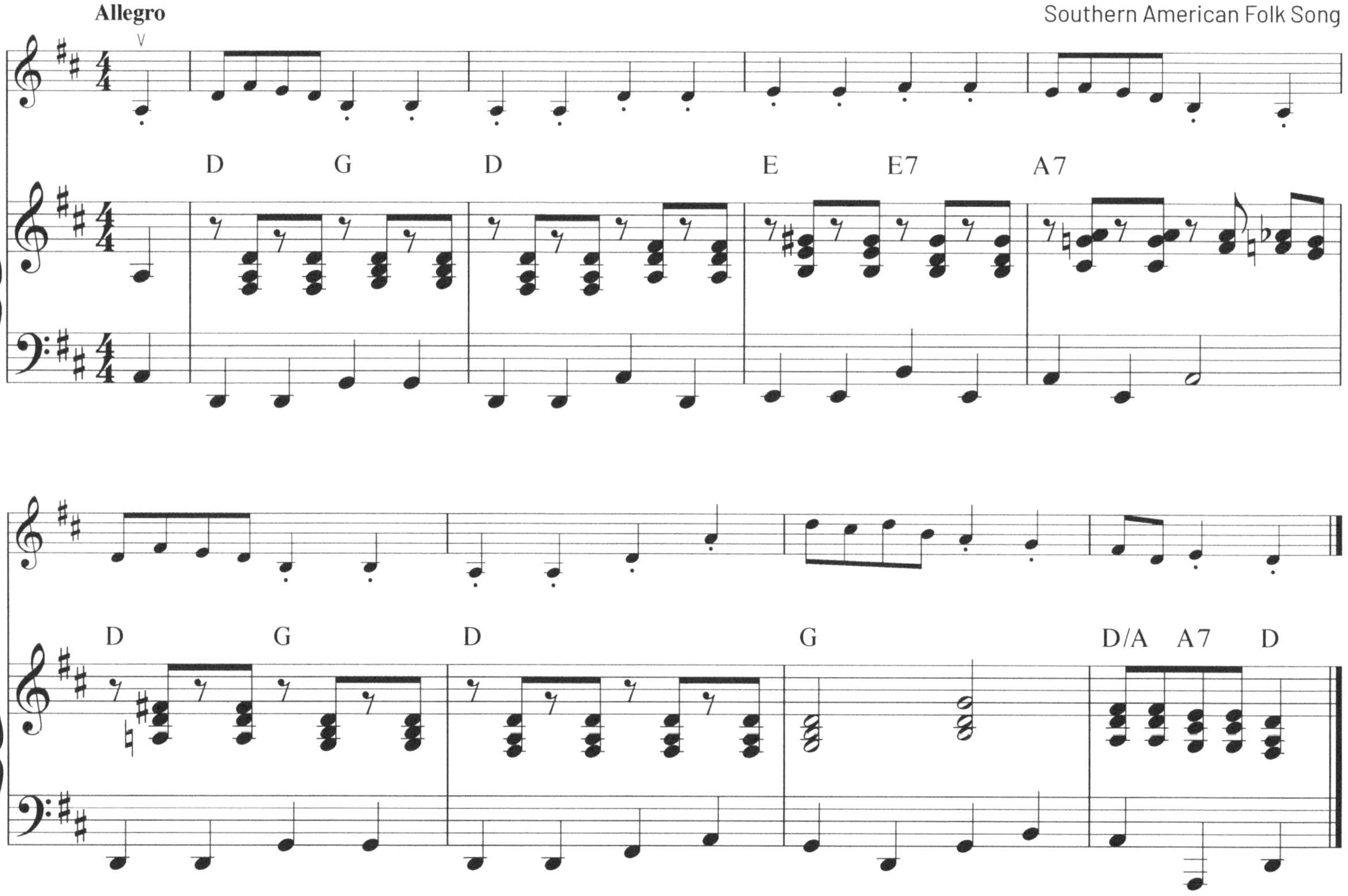

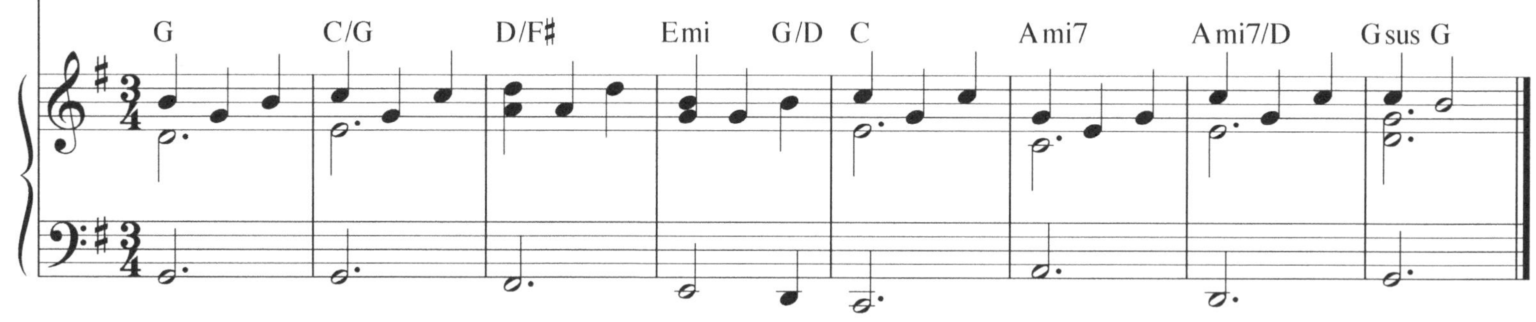

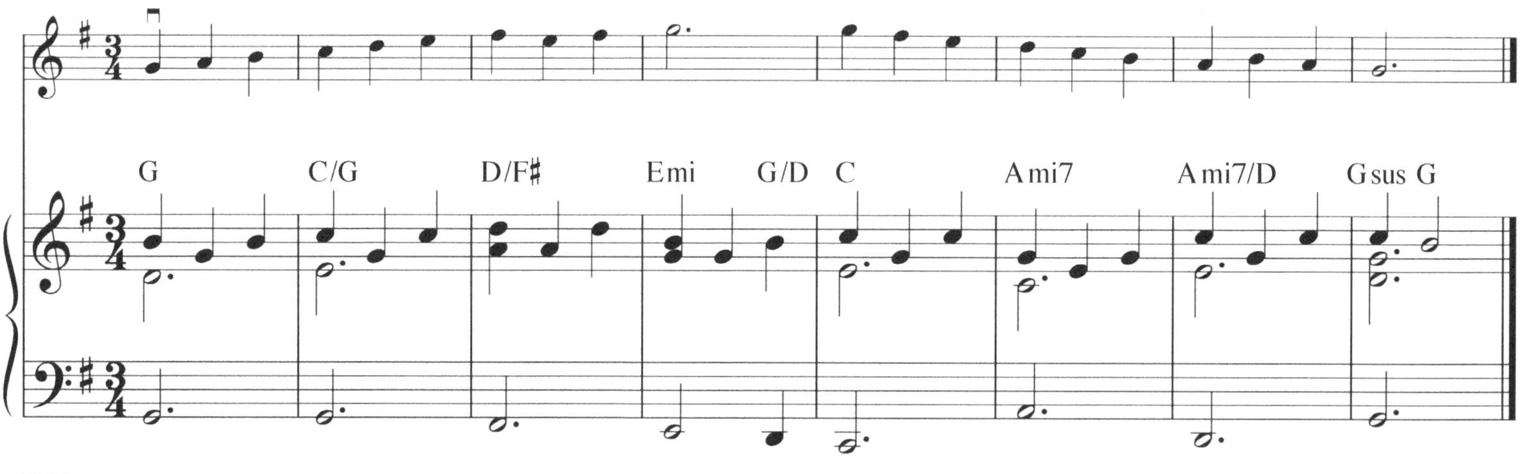

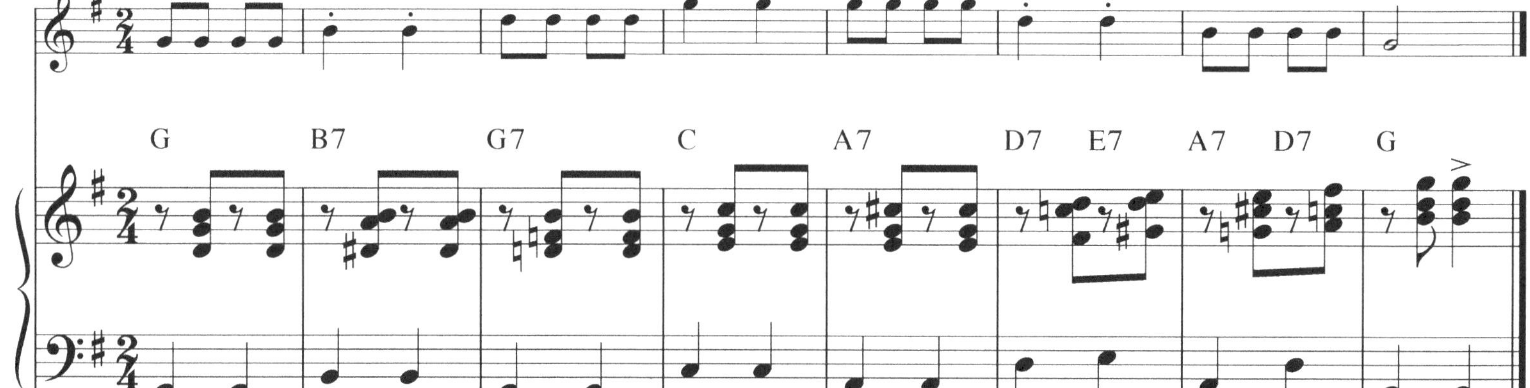

171.

G
C/G
G
Ami/C
G/D
D/F♯
G
Emi
D/E
Emi
Ami
G/A
Ami/G
D/F♯
Ami/D
D7
G
172.
G
G/B
C
D
C
Ami7
C/D
G
173.
G
D
G
D
C
D6
D7
G

174. HOOKED ON D MAJOR

175. WALTZING BOWS

176. POP GOES THE WEASEL

177.
C
G7
C
Emi
F
G7
Dmi
G7
C
178.
C
F
C
G7
C
179.
C
Emi
F
G
Ami
G/F
F
Emi
Dmi
G6
G7
C
180.
Ami
Emi
Dmi
Ami
F
G7
F
G7
C

181. FORTE AND PIANO

182. SURPRISE SYMPHONY THEME

183. D MAJOR

D
G
D
A
Student books have repeats, not 1st and 2nd endings.
1.
2.
D
Bmi
G
D
D
184. G MAJOR
G
C
G
D
Student books have repeats, not 1st and 2nd endings.
1.
2.
G
Emi
C
G
G

185. G MAJOR

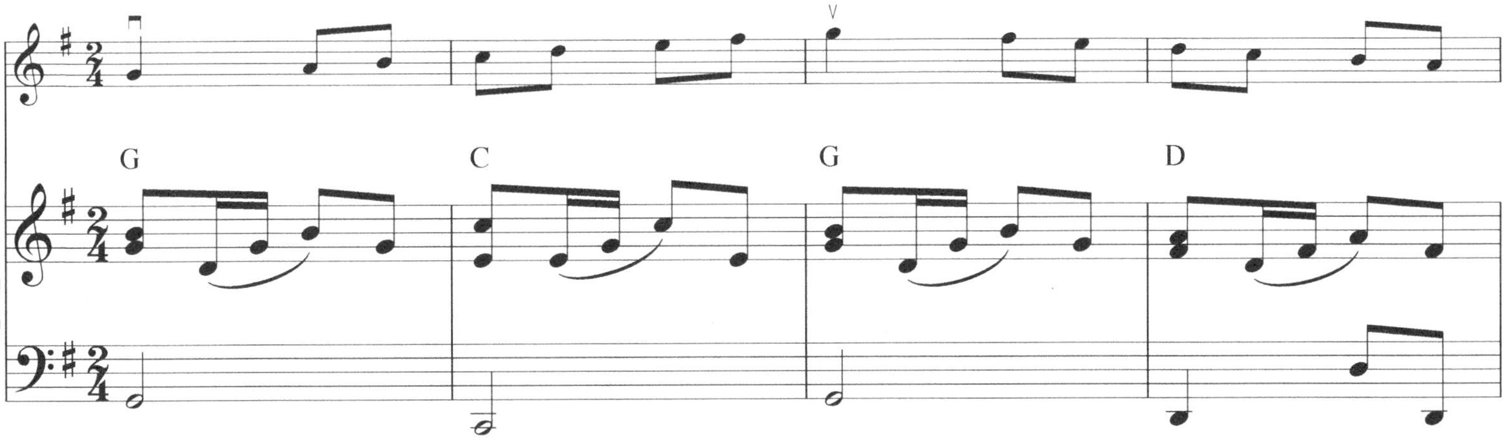

G C G D

Student books have repeats, not 1st and 2nd endings.

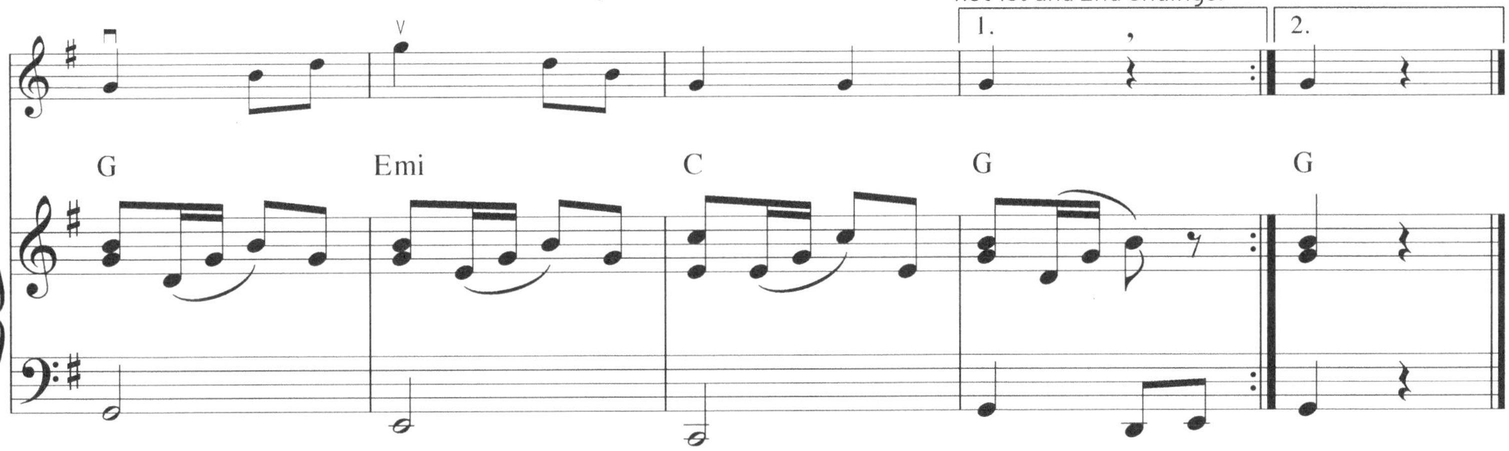

1. 2.

G Emi C G G

186. C MAJOR

187. C MAJOR

Student books have repeats, not 1st and 2nd endings.

188. CRIPPLE CREEK – Orchestra Arrangement (A = Melody and B = Harmony)

American Folk Song
Arr. Michael Allen

Allegro

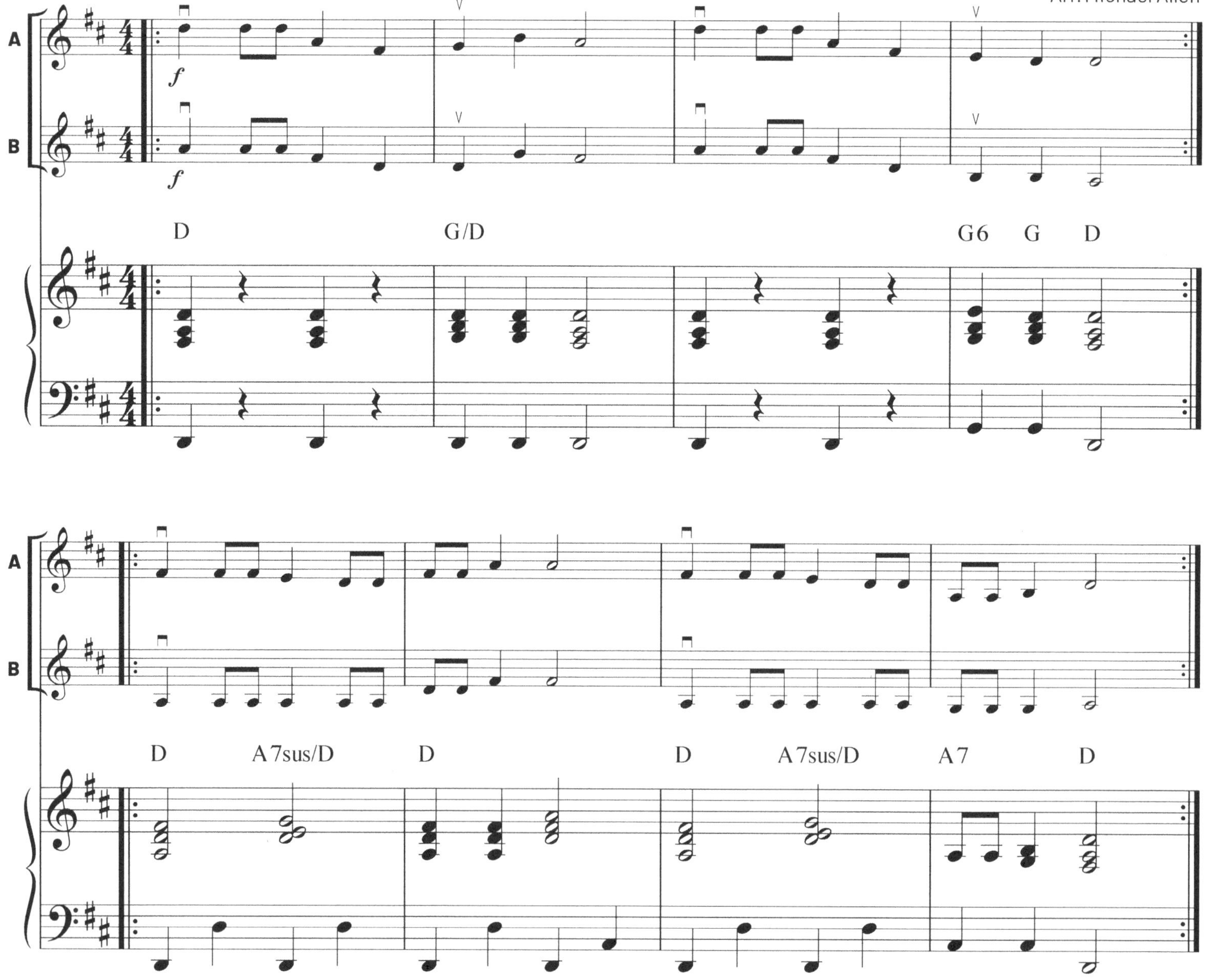

A
B
f
f

D G/D G6 G D

A
B

D A7sus/D D D A7sus/D A7 D

189. TEKELE LOMERIA – Orchestra Arrangement

Kenyan Warrior Song
Arr. John Higgins

190. WILLIAM TELL OVERTURE – Orchestra Arrangement

Gioachino Rossini
Arr. John Higgins

191. ROCKIN' STRINGS – Orchestra Arrangement

192. SIMPLE GIFTS – Orchestra Arrangement

Shaker Folk Song
Arr. John Higgins

A
B
D
D/G5
A5
A
G
Emi7
D
N.C.
opt.
19
D
D/C♯
Bmi7
D/A
G6/9
D/F♯
A/G
D
Gma7
D/F♯
Emi7
D
G6
A
G
Emi7
D
Ped.

193. MINUET NO. 1 – Violin Solo

Johann Sebastian Bach
Arr. John Higgins

193. MINUET IN C – Viola Solo

Johann Sebastian Bach
Arr. John Higgins

193. MINUET NO. 2 – Cello Solo

Johann Sebastian Bach
Arr. John Higgins

193. MARCH IN D – Double Bass Solo

Johann Sebastian Bach
Arr. John Higgins

194. RHYTHM JAM – *Student books have an improvisation exercise.*

195. INSTANT MELODY – *Student books have an improvisation exercise.*